WAKING UP A LEADER

WAKING
UP
A LEADER

FIVE RELATIONSHIPS
OF SUCCESS

DR. DAPHNE SCOTT

LIONCREST
PUBLISHING

WAKING UP A LEADER

Five Relationships of Success

ISBN   978-1-5445-0484-1 *Hardcover*

978-1-5445-0482-7 *Paperback*

978-1-5445-0483-4 *Ebook*

978-1-5445-0485-8 *Audiobook*

To all leaders and beings everywhere, whose
inner knowing always knows the way.

CONTENTS

INTRODUCTION

Let me tell you a story about an ambitious thirty-year-old physical therapist. We'll call her Daphne, because that's her name. After receiving a degree in physical therapy, Daphne started treating patients and found she was quite skilled. Soon she earned a promotion and took on a leadership position at the company where she worked. At the same time that she was leading teams and treating patients, Daphne decided to pursue clinical research, which meant writing and publishing papers. She continued to climb the corporate ladder, becoming regional manager, then director of leadership development, then director of clinical outcomes, at which point she had three clinics reporting to her.

Yet, somehow, it wasn't quite enough. Daphne was still aspiring and decided it was time to get a doctorate of science in physical therapy, as well as two certifications in executive coaching. She also began pursuing her own leadership development business, supporting other leaders through coaching and speaking engagements, outside her full-time job. By then, Daphne was a fellow in the American Academy of Orthopedic Manual Physical Therapists, a board-certified orthopedic specialist, and a partner in her company. She was making more money than she ever thought possible.

And she was miserable.

Okay, *I* was miserable. For over ten years, I had worked and studied and sacrificed. I had achieved a high level of professional success, but my relationship with my partner started eroding, I hadn't seen my family or friends with any regularity, and all of my plants were dead. I had gained fifteen pounds, and I woke up every two hours each night with anxiety and mild panic attacks. I was stressed out, I couldn't relax, and I didn't know what to do.

WAKING UP TO ME

As a healthcare professional, I knew that medicating myself to sleep wasn't the answer, but I didn't know what the answer was. In a last-ditch effort, I googled "how to manage stress" and stumbled upon a meditation website. I was a little skeptical that sitting and doing nothing could take away my stress, but I was desperate, so I decided to give it a try. I took a six-week introductory meditation class at a Buddhist center in Chicago, then practiced haphazardly for the next eighteen months.

Through meditation and learning some necessary leadership skills, I slowly realized a truth that changed my personal and professional life. It was that my stress and anxiety hadn't resulted purely from situations, circumstances, or people, but from the way I was relating to those things. In other words, the problem wasn't something outside me—the problem was within me.

The good news was this: if the problem stemmed from something inside me, then so did the solution. Over the next year, I continued waking up to a new way of thinking and relating that resulted in more peace, joy, and well-being, and I started coaching my clients to do the same.

There was just one problem: I also stayed in the career that had brought me more stress than joy and had led me to hit rock bottom.

I knew I didn't want that life. I knew I needed to make a change. But I was terrified. My work was my identity. Who would I be without my title and position? How would I ever make as much money somewhere else?

At the root was fear of the unknown. I chose the familiar and yet miserable because I didn't know what would happen if I walked into my boss's office and quit. Ultimately, integrity forced me to take a chance. I couldn't stand that I was coaching people to live their best lives and explore what was possible when I wasn't doing it myself.

So, I quit my corporate job and started my own business. I also left my relationship. My new life wasn't immediately filled with rainbows and unicorns. I created a big mess and disappointed a lot of people, but it was something I had to do. In the end, it was totally worth it.

FIVE KEY RELATIONSHIPS

Does my story of misery and stress sound familiar? Are you working too many hours, neglecting friends, and sacrificing your health in the name of professional success? If so, you're not alone. Many organizational leaders share this experience, even multimillionaires like Arianna Huffington, who passed out from sheer exhaustion, hit her face on her desk, and woke up in a pool of her own blood.

As I discovered, the solution is first found within. As leaders, we spend a lot of time and energy trying to control our external world. We talk about being productive, we buy eighty planners and fifty calendars, we might even attend meditation retreats or spend weekends away in the woods—and then wonder why these things don't make us more productive or, at minimum, less stressed. It's like weeding a garden: if we only pull off the tops, the weeds quickly grow back. To effect real change, we need to get to the root—our inner life. External actions will follow, and they will be much more effective. That time in the woods or using a planner will have the desired end.

At the same time, however, leaders do need to consciously learn transactional skills to effectively lead and manage others. This is the "yes and" of leadership: we must transform the internal without ignoring the external. We need both.

Most leadership books focus solely on the transactional skills involved in managing: planning projects, organizing schedules, forecasting budgets, and so on. Some focus on transformational skills to help leaders renew their vision and better themselves. Few leadership books, however, cover both planes: transforming the way leaders see the world, their businesses, and themselves, while simultaneously helping them transact skillfully in the workplace. This is one of those books.

Through my own inner growth and experience coaching clients, I came to see that we all have five key relationships that require our attention if we want to thrive:

1. Time
2. Money
3. The self
4. Friendships
5. The unknown

How we manage these relationships dictates our well-being. In this book, we'll explore how you can maximize your full potential through each relationship. You'll learn the transformational (internal) and transactional (external) leadership skills that will help you become a more effective leader. You'll discover new ways to use thought, feeling, and mindful attention to become more comfortable within yourself and in the world around you.

A NEW WAY OF RELATING AND LEADING

When life isn't going our way, our default as humans is to blame the external world—the things happening outside us. This book will challenge you to look inside for the source of your present unhappiness, frustration, stress, or dissatisfaction. Doing so will take work. Internal change isn't a quick fix. But if you approach this book as a guide with a sense of vulnerability and willingness to be truthful about what's causing your discontent, you'll reap the rewards personally and professionally.

I have lived and tested these concepts as a formerly

stressed-out, miserable leader who found a way to bridge the internal and external with a deep sense of peace, calm, and self-worth. I worked in corporate America for twenty years, leading teams and managing people. For the past fifteen years, I have coached others through the concepts I describe here. However, this book is grounded not only in my own experience but also in research and real-world examples of these transformational and transactional skills in action.

As leaders, we make decisions that impact the hopes, dreams, and aspirations of other people. That's a huge responsibility. Learning to manage the five key relationships from a place of trust instead of fear will decrease your stress and anxiety, improve your well-being, and enable you to make the best decisions for yourself and your team.

Have you suffered enough? If so, a new way of relating and leading awaits.

PART I

WHAT YOU NEED TO SUCCEED

"We lead people. We manage things."

—GRACE HOPPER, UNITED STATES NAVY REAR
ADMIRAL AND COMPUTER SCIENTIST

The terms *transactional leadership* and *transformational leadership* come from James Burns and Bernard Bass. According to Burns and Bass, transactional leadership involves interaction for the purpose of getting things done. "Transactional leaders mostly consider how to marginally improve and maintain the quantity and quality of performance, how to substitute one goal for another, and how to reduce resistance to particular actions and then how to implement decisions."[1]

Transformational leadership, on the other hand, concerns mindset, values, and vision. It involves raising "colleagues, subordinates, and clients to a greater awareness about the issues, especially the issues of consequence."[2] Transformational leaders' yardstick for measuring success is much bigger than the financial bottom line. They seek to support the overall well-being of those they lead.

In today's workplace, leaders need both skillsets. They need to keep a schedule, plan a budget, and communicate effectively with their team. At the same time, they need to manage their inner life and support others in doing the same. Transactional skills give leaders the ability to deal with the external who, what, when, and how. Transformational skills enable leaders to understand their internal why—the ultimate meaning, purpose, and vision behind their transacting—and cultivate environments in which people can do their best work and flourish.

In Part I, we'll discuss the transformational, ultimate truths we need to grasp to help us transact more skillfully in the conventional world of business. Chapter 1 discusses the idea of relating and what we really mean by relationships. Chapters 2 and 3 focus on paying attention: what it means, why we need to, and how to train ourselves to do so. As hinted at in the introduction, paying attention is the key skill for relating from a different internal place. Chapter 4 discusses thoughts and emotions and provides insight into developing a healthy relationship with both. Each chapter ends with an exercise to help you practice the skills presented.

In Part II, we'll discuss the five key relationships and the transformational and transactional skills leaders need to "wake up" to engage in a new way of leading.

You may be wondering, "Can I read about the five key relationships in Part II without reading the transformational discussion in Part I?"

Yes, but I wouldn't recommend it. This book is all about waking up to how we relate to our world, and the first four chapters set the groundwork and specifics for changing our internal response to external people, circumstances, and events. Part I is essential to what comes next.

CHAPTER 1

WHAT DO I MEAN BY *RELATIONSHIPS?*

"For there is nothing either good or bad, but thinking makes it so."

—WILLIAM SHAKESPEARE, *HAMLET*

You're sitting in your favorite chair with your beverage of choice, reading this book. What is your sense of time right now? Do you feel like you have plenty of time to read today, or do you feel rushed and short on time?

It's Saturday afternoon and you're walking the dog. What is the weather like today? Is it too hot or too cold?

You walk into the office on Monday morning and survey the week's workload. Do you have too much work on your plate right now or too little?

In all three of these scenarios, your response to the questions indicates your relationship to the thing. The items themselves—time, weather, and work—are neutral. They aren't good or bad, and they aren't doing anything to you. They are simply showing up as what they are: the time of day, the temperature, and the work sitting on your desk.

Time, for instance, is just the hour on the clock. Three o'clock is no better or worse than four o'clock, and two o'clock doesn't act any differently than one o'clock. Time only takes on a different meaning in our minds based on how we relate to it. Consider two people sitting side by side for ten minutes. One person is casually reading her book, while the other person is holding a ten-pound weight overhead. They experience the same ten minutes in two very different ways.

The same variety of experience applies to work or the weather. If it's ninety degrees outside, one person might be happy because the heat eases his arthritis, whereas the other person might be miserable. If it's raining, some people will love the cozy feeling of being inside and listening to the storm, and other people will hate it because they don't like the dismal, gray sky and getting wet. Same weather, very different experiences.

We tend to think that objects, people, and events outside ourselves cause us to feel a certain way. This simply isn't true. Our internal reaction determines our initial experience, whether positive or negative, and we can learn to respond versus simply react.[1] We can choose how we relate to our world. Learning this transformational skill will enable you to transact with others more skillfully. It will also change your life in whimsical and magical ways.

When we become aware of our naturally occurring reactivity, we can choose to respond differently. This is important since our relationships and the skillfulness of our actions are first and foremost born from how we relate.

RELATIONSHIPS AND RELATING

In essence, a *relationship* is made up of an action that occurs between us and something in our world. It describes how we are *relating* to the other person or phenomenon, consciously or unconsciously. We are always relating to people, places, events, objects, ourselves—anything encountered through our five senses and also our thoughts.

Try the following activity:

1. Look at an object in the room where you're sitting. It could be anything—a lamp, your cat, the rug.
2. As soon as your eyes make contact with the object,

take note of your reaction. It will fall in one of three categories: *positive* ("I like that thing. That's pleasant."), *negative* ("I don't like that thing. That's unpleasant."), or *neutral* (no reaction, indifference, as if you're not even noticing the thing).

3. Repeat the exercise with a few different objects in the room, and notice how your internal reaction varies.

This exercise illustrates a transformational truth that will come up throughout our discussion. We react to *everything,* and we always react in one of three ways—pleasant, unpleasant, or neutral.[2] The preceding exercise used the sense of sight, but the same applies to all of our senses. Whenever we see, hear, taste, touch, smell, or even think something, we react. The nature of our reaction depends on several causes and conditions, including context, which we will discuss next.

CONTEXT

If you give five dollars to a ten-year-old, the child is probably going to think he's rich. If you give five dollars to an adult making $100,000 a year, she will not be so impressed. In either case, five dollars is just five dollars. It's neutral and has no inherent influence on the person's reaction. The relationship between the person and external phenomena, such as money, flows out of the individual's context, or the mindset from which he or she is relating to the thing encountered.

At the very root, we relate from one of two contexts: fear or trust. Fear is based on the desire to make things permanent. On the one hand, fear involves avoiding. We want to avoid losing what we have. Fear also involves holding on to or not losing the things we have. When we respond from fear, it's as if one closed fist holds on while the other open hand pushes away. In this fear-based context, we experience stress and tension, and neither hand is very useful.

Trust, on the other hand, is characterized by openness, balance, and a willingness to engage fully with the stuff of life. We have two open hands, ready to receive whatever shows up. The trust-based context involves greater peace and calm, too, regardless of what we encounter. Who doesn't want to experience more of that? Our operating context often creates our reality without us even realizing what's happening. We react to everything in our world. To become skillful in working with these reactions, we need to see where they're coming from. If we don't pay attention, we can start believing that our reactions are actually caused by things. Then we start believing that the only way to have a different relationship with something is for the thing to change. We might think, "If only my team member would change. Then I would finally be happy." In truth, what needs to change is our context—our unconscious mindset and way of relating.

At the root of fear is the sense that our identity, and therefore our well-being, is somehow being threatened. Father Thomas Keating was a Catholic monk who revised the idea of Christian contemplative practices. He wrote a welcoming prayer in which he identified a way to make this perceived threat seem far less significant: let go of security, control, and approval.[3] In other words, when we let go of believing that those three things come from outside of us, we experience greater levels of trust. We begin to see that our sense of approval, for example, needn't come from other people or external situations.

When we believe that the external world is solely in charge of our well-being, we suffer. We immediately feel that things should be different than they are: "I should have more time than I do," or "I should have less time so I'm not bored." We think that if things were different (having more or less time), we would be happy, secure, affirmed, and in control. Not so. We are actually the ones creating our own suffering and discomfort by resisting reality. We need to see how we are relating first. Then we can choose from wisdom and compassion—the two wings of mindfulness—what our next action (if any) needs to be.

HALF FULL OR HALF EMPTY?

You're probably familiar with the idea of seeing a glass as half full or half empty. Seeing the glass as half full is generally associated with having a positive outlook on life, while seeing the glass as half empty is linked with negativity. However, the realists among us may stomp their feet in protest. The other half of the glass is, in fact, empty.

What about the less-than-savory things that occur in our business and life? Do we simply ignore them? Not at all. Relating from trust doesn't mean we ignore the unsavory or leave problems unaddressed. This is likely one of the biggest misunderstandings about mindfulness. Living mindfully involves action. It doesn't mean ignoring life's trials and tribulations or giving too much attention to things beyond our control (as most things are).

The first step in relating to the glass is to see that it's a glass. Like the weather, time, and work, the glass isn't good or bad; it's neutral.

Next, we need to appreciate the context and understand that we are relating to this innocuous glass as either half empty or half full. Both ways of seeing have their benefits as well as their perils. If I only see the glass as half full, then I may not be addressing issues that need to be addressed. Conversely, if I only see the glass as half empty, then I may not be aware of the good things that are occurring. I may not see that I can cultivate positive things in life that can be helpful and joyful to myself and others.

Here's a story to illustrate this point. A mother sent her son to the market with money to buy a bottle of oil. On his way back home, the boy fell and spilled half the bottle of oil. He was very upset and cried to his mother that he only had half a bottle left. What a terrible day!

The next week, the mother sent her second son to buy oil, likely hoping for better results. As luck would have it, this son also fell and spilled half of the bottle of oil. His reaction, however, was different. He celebrated with his mother because he saved half the bottle of oil. He was so lucky!

Finally, the mother sent her last son to buy a bottle of oil. He went to the market and had the bottle filled to the rim. Alas, he, too, fell and spilled half of the bottle of oil. This boy had a wiser, more balanced perspective. He came to his mother grateful that he still had half a bottle of oil left, but he also understood that half of the oil had spilled on the ground. He saw the full reality of the bottle as half full *and* half empty. The boy knew just what he needed to do. He went back to the market to work and earn the money he would need to fill the bottle to the rim again.[4]

When we relate to people and circumstances from a place of fear, we first lose sight of the reality that the glass is simply a glass. It isn't doing anything. It isn't good or bad. It just is. Even if we are able to see the glass being half full, fear drives us to hold on to what we have. We become attached and fear losing it all, so much so that we forget we could as easily refill the glass completely if needed. In addition, fear can cause us to see the glass as half empty and become stuck in seeing only what's missing or not going well. We then spend our time attempting to mitigate all of the bad stuff, avoiding life, and desperately trying to hold on to what we have.

When we operate from a place of trust, however, we view the glass as half full and half empty. We see the full glass. We focus on what we have, what we want to remove, and what we want to add to or cultivate in our lives. In other words, we practice a balanced meliorism. Meliorism is the idea that the world can be made better by human effort. When we view the glass from a place of trust, our human effort involves both removing the negative (mitigative meliorism) and adding the positive (constructive meliorism).

When we're suffering, we often look for what we can get rid of to stop the suffering and make our lives better. If someone is in a toxic, unhealthy relationship or if a business discovers its practices are harming the envient, it would seem wise to take mitigative action.

moving the bad doesn't necessarily mean we start experiencing the good. We need to make a conscious effort to add the positive. Life is about taking wise action, removing the negative and cultivating the good as we are able.[5]

The glass of water is what it is. The difference comes from how we choose to see it. The point isn't to avoid looking at our fear. The point is to realize when we get stuck in fear, when all we're doing is avoiding things or resisting reality. This wisdom starts with being aware of the context from which we are relating.

WOULD YOU LIKE EGGS?

Scenario 1: A woman opens her eyes, stretches, and turns toward the person lying next to her. She snuggles closer and whispers, "Would you like eggs for breakfast this morning?"

Scenario 2: A teenager stomps into the kitchen, grabs a pan out of the cabinet, and slams it onto the stove. Then he asks the younger sibling seated at the table, "Would you like eggs for breakfast this morning?"

The same words are spoken in both scenarios. Are they spoken in the same tone of voice or with the same meaning or intentionality? Probably not. This is how context works. The words themselves don't matter as much as the context from which we speak them. Remember the old adage, "It isn't what you say that matters. It's how you say it"? That applies here.

Leaders often ask me for a script they can use during performance reviews with team members. I tell them it won't help. I can give someone the exact words, but if they are spoken in anger or frustration, the employee will know. Those same words will come out very differently if spoken from a place of trust with clear intentions.

If a manager tries to give performance feedback from a fear-based context, this might show up as the manager being most interested in controlling the employee's reaction. In an effort to avoid upsetting the employee, the manager might soften her words or withhold direct comments that could ultimately help the employee perform better. A manager with this mindset has lost sight of the main reason for sharing the feedback, which is to support her employee's well-being and what he can learn from the experience to perform better. Instead, the manager's context is one of controlling and avoiding due to fear.

On the other hand, if a manager speaks from a place of trust, she will be most interested in helping the employee succeed. She will provide the necessary feedback, even it makes her uncomfortable or upsets the employee. She will deliver the feedback with the best intentions and in the most skillful manner she can create, knowing the employee's reaction is beyond her control. A manager with this mindset is open to whatever happens. Her greatest intention is to support the employee in doing his best work, not controlling his reaction.

TALKING TO OURSELVES

Anytime our well-being feels threatened, we tend to see the world (our glass) as half empty, and we often find ourselves spinning in circles. We then start relating to people, places, events, and thoughts from a fear-based context. Stress, anxiety, and other negative emotions follow and further threaten our sense of well-being. We have thus added a second arrow to the first—an already less-than-preferred moment.[6]

How we "talk" to ourselves at this point is key. The answer isn't to merely think positively or pretend the glass is half full when it's not. When our well-being is threatened and we start operating out of fear, we need to admit that something is happening so we can address it. But as we've seen, often that something isn't the external event. It's our reaction to it.

Learning to talk to yourself about what is happening

in the moment and what may happen in the future is a key transformational skill. We will refer to this concept throughout the book. For now, I will provide a few options for effectively talking to yourself when you are relating from fear.

Objective Reality versus Subjective Experience

One option is to remind yourself that there's a difference between external, objective reality, or what a video camera would record, and our internal, subjective experience and interpretations. For example, if I'm sitting on my porch and I see a white egret walking toward the pond, that is an external, objective condition. Let's say the egret walks past an alligator and then flies off. That's still an external, objective condition. However, if I think the egret took off because the gator scared it, then I've moved into subjective experience. I'm now making up a story in my head to explain the external, objective event I witnessed.

We tend to think our subjective experience is the full representation of reality. We believe the thoughts we think and our interpretation of external events are the truth. They're usually not. Recognizing this truth can bring us back to the present and help us shift how we're relating to our current situation. This also makes our conversations with others and also ourselves much easier to navigate. The poet David Whyte wrote, "All of life is just one big conversation."[7] We have conversations with ourselves and with other people simultaneously. The conversation I have with myself is born from the way I relate to things and how I view and interpret what's going on externally. However, our internal conversations are not fully reality. They are thoughts, interpretations, and stories often born of our past experience. Most often, they do not reflect what is truly happening in the objective, external, transactional world.

Permanent, Personal, and Pervasive

We often relate from fear in the face of unpredictable, external happenings in our world. One way to talk to ourselves at these moments can be summarized as the three Ps. This approach was first described by Dr. Martin Seligman in his book *Learned Optimism*.[8] The deeper truth of the three Ps as it relates to impermanence comes from much of Buddhist teachings.

The first P is *permanent*. Learn to recognize that nothing is permanent. Everything comes and goes. By paying attention to our moment-by-moment experience, we can watch feelings, thoughts, and events arise and fall away. We will thus experience impermanence in reality as well as understand it intellectually.

Next, understand that nothing is *personal*. Everyone

experiences pleasure and pain, gain and loss. No one is immune. The experience of fear or anger or feeling slighted by another human is not unique to you. All beings experience these things. All beings also desire to feel love.

Lastly, understand that nothing is *pervasive*. Something happening in one area of your life doesn't necessarily mean that it will impact all areas of your life, or at least not in the same way. We will return to the three Ps later in greater depth. For now, it's enough to practice them as you relate to things in and around you.

Self-Distancing

You'll probably find that shifting your context is harder in some situations, depending on how threatened you feel. When you're really struggling to unhook yourself from a fear-based mindset, try a self-distancing technique. To give yourself perspective on the transient nature of the event, ask yourself, "How will I see this event in five years?" It most likely won't hold the same intensity. Asking yourself this question will also help you remember that everything changes.[9]

CHAINED TO THE DOT

As we've seen so far, we relate to things in life consciously or unconsciously and from a place of trust or fear. Fear keeps us where we've always been: familiar but miserable. Although we seem to be moving forward, we are essentially chained to the dot, running around and around in a circle (figure 1.1). In an effort to avoid one scenario and move on to another that we think will relieve our suffering, we unconsciously repeat the same behavior and thought patterns over and over. In the end, however, we find ourselves right back where we started.

When we choose to step into trust, we break the chain and leave the dot. We step fully into the world of possibility, and also the unknown. Our actions take on new life. From here, we can learn the art of being intentional and skillful.

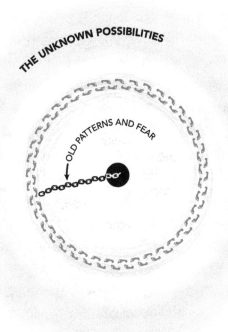

THE UNKNOWN POSSIBILITIES

OLD PATTERNS AND FEAR

Figure 1.1. When we're chained to the dot, we miss all the other possible choices for action. We're unable to step into the unknown.

INTENTIONS AND SKILLFULNESS

Imagine it's the end of the year. I'm looking at my company's quarterly financials, and I realize we have done very well. In Scenario 1, I decide to give everyone a bonus as a reward for their hard work. I want to share the monetary success with my team, and I know they will all be very appreciative.

In Scenario 2, it's again the end of the year, and the

company has done well financially. I decide to give out bonuses, but not because I know my team would appreciate it and I want to share the success. It's because I want them to keep working hard and make even more money next quarter because this will reflect well on me.

In Scenario 3, it's the end of the year, the company has done well, and I decide to hand out bonuses based on performance. Those who didn't contribute as much to the company's success won't receive as much money. I don't want to talk to the underperformers directly because I want to avoid conflict, but I know my team will discuss how much money they received. I'm hoping the underachievers' disappointment will motivate them to step up and start working harder.

If you were to watch a video of all three scenarios, my action would look exactly the same. In all three cases I am giving out bonus checks. What you don't see are my intentions behind the action.

In Scenario 1, I'm operating from a context of trust and openness, which creates my intention of sharing the success and supporting my team in getting their monetary needs met. In Scenarios 2 and 3, I'm operating from fear. In Scenario 2, I'm trying to manipulate my team into continuing the hard work, maybe because I'm afraid they won't do so out of intrinsic motivation. For my own benefit, I need them to keep the behavior going. In Scenario 3, I'm acting out of a need to avoid conflict and maintain personal comfort. How we relate creates our intentions, and our actions spring from those intentions.

Let's go back to Scenario 1, where I want to give bonuses as a reward for hard work. I realize I have only enough money to give bonuses to the top two performers on the team. Even though my intention is to reward hard work, it may not be skillful for me to offer bonuses to two people since everyone contributed, even if, in my opinion, those contributions don't seem equal. Rewarding two out of twenty may create discord.

Good intentions are not enough. We also need to be skillful in our actions. This is where the transformational and transactional meet. Internally, we need to wake up to how we're relating and choose to relate from trust. We also need to direct our good intentions, as best we can, into skillful actions that support the well-being of others.

THE TRANSIENT AND IMPERMANENT NATURE OF LIFE

As you've been reading this book, you've likely noticed different thoughts coming into your awareness. Perhaps you've had an anxiety-provoking thought or one that made you smile. Where are those thoughts now? Maybe you've also heard sounds in the background, a dog barking or a car starting. Where are those sounds now?

As we learn to pay attention (stay tuned for more in chapters 2 and 3) and to be fully awake, we begin to understand and experience the deepest truth of our existence: nothing is permanent.[10] Thoughts come and go. Circumstances change. Our emotions rise and fall away. Sensations appear unbidden. Like clouds in the sky, they float right by, changing shape and disappearing altogether.

As mentioned in the Talking to Ourselves section, reminding ourselves that life is impermanent is one key for unhooking ourselves from a pattern of fear. Everything comes and goes, so there is nothing to worry about. The situation at hand will not be as it is forever. This, too, shall pass. When you're relating from fear, these little reminders can work like magic and bring you the peace you seek. This place of trust and openness is also where wise choices are born. How we relate to the impermanent and transient nature of life directly influences the way we transact with others in our personal and professional lives and the way we see the world at large.

Being aware of how we're relating is of the essence. This awareness comes from the daily practice of mindfulness, or learning to pay attention to the truth of what arises in each moment. We will discuss this core truth next.

EXERCISE: THE INVENTORY OF COMPLAINTS

Goal: This exercise will help you identify the external phenomena you relate to from a place of fear rather than trust.

Process: Write down all the areas of your life where you have been complaining. Consider all aspects of your life, personal and professional. For example, do you complain about not getting enough sleep or exercise? Do you complain about not being smart enough or not having time to take classes? This is simply an exercise in exploration, so write down anything that comes to mind without judgment. You might bucket these complaints within the five key relationships of time, money, the self, friendships, and the unknown.

As you think through areas of your life, notice whether you feel constriction or tightness. Notice what complaining feels like in your body.

The key question here is, what unmet need is this complaint showing you? How is fear keeping you from getting your need(s) met? What stories do you tell yourself that keep you from addressing the complaint? How are you stuck on the dot and repeating the same pattern?

If you would like to access the Inventory of Complaints handout, please go to www.wakingupaleader.com.

CHAPTER 2

PAYING ATTENTION, PART ONE

WHAT IT IS AND WHY WE NEED TO

"Attention is the most basic form of love. Through it we bless and are blessed."

—JOHN TARRANT, ZEN TEACHER AND AUTHOR

I was working with the HR team at Company X. The day before, a disgruntled employee posted negative comments about the company on Glassdoor. I listened to the team voice their concerns about how they were going to end up in a lawsuit and suffer innumerable horrid things as a result of this post. After letting them circle for about fifteen minutes, I said, "Tell me the facts."

They all stopped talking and looked at me as though I hadn't been listening. Then Naomi asked, "What?"

"Tell me the facts. What would a video camera record?"

Naomi replied, "The employee said she was unhappy about working here and claimed she was sexually harassed. She went so far as to say there's a culture of sexual harassment here."

"Okay," I said. "Now, what are you all upset about?"

"We could end up in a lawsuit because of this!" Naomi exclaimed. "And we could look really bad to people who may be thinking about working here."

"Where is that concern coming from?"

They all looked at each other until Amy finally said, "Fear."

"Right. So, what has actually happened?"

"Well, she posted those comments," Naomi said.

"Is that it?"

"Yes."

"It's true that you would have preferred she didn't post those accusations, but nothing else has happened so far, right?"

"Yeah, but other people are going to read this," Mike said.

"Has anybody contacted you yet?" They all shook their heads. "And when did this happen?"

"Yesterday at noon," Mike replied.

"And it's nine o'clock in the morning. So, between yesterday at noon and today at nine, has anything happened?"

"Not really," Naomi admitted, "except that we've been talking about it nonstop."

I watched the group slowly grasp my point. They had worked themselves into a panic over many things that hadn't even happened. They were giving all of their attention to catastrophizing thoughts about the future. They were not paying attention to the present facts or how they were relating. As a result, they were reacting directly from fear and creating a lot of anxiety for themselves.

They all sat in silence for a minute. Then the vice president laughed and said, "I guess what's really true is that nothing has happened. And what's true for me is that I would like to ask her more questions. I want to get a sense of what is really happening. Is this a global issue we need to address, or is this someone's individual cry for help?"

"Do you think there's anything we need to manage from a PR perspective?" Ruby asked. "Is there messaging we need to get out to the company?"

"It's one person's comment, so maybe we need to let people know that we're going to investigate," Mike suggested.

The energy in the room had completely shifted. They were no longer in a lathered frenzy. Instead they were talking through next steps, and in under five minutes, they had a plan with two action items.

Once they started paying attention to the facts in front of them, they calmed down and became productive. They didn't spin for days and create more work for themselves and more drama. They were more intentional and skillful in their actions. Had they reacted from the context of their fear and panic, their actions could have cost the team and the company more energy, time, and money.

If we want to be mindful, awake leaders, we need to pay attention. We need to intentionally focus on the present—

not be dragged back into the regretful past or shoved into the anxious future. This chapter explores what it means to pay attention and why we need to use this transformational skill in our workplace transactions.

WHAT IS PAYING ATTENTION?

In essence, paying attention is mindfulness. It involves consciously keeping our attention in the present moment, on the facts in front of us. Paying attention means focusing on what's happening right now, not what happened in the past or might happen in the future.

Jon Kabat-Zinn, PhD, is one of the pioneers who brought mindfulness into mainstream Western society. He defines mindfulness as "paying attention in a particular way, on purpose, in the present moment and nonjudgmentally."[1] The key to mindfulness is seeing how we're relating to our judgmental nature, which decides what we believe is good or bad based on what we like or don't like. Judgment is simply a particular type of thought, and as we've learned, thoughts are transient. We need to see judgment for what it is, acknowledge it, and let it go, rather than fighting it or judging our judging.

When we're present, we don't judge our experience as good and try to hang on to it, nor do we judge it as bad and try to get rid of it. We just accept the momentary experience as it is. If we happen to see judgment arising, we can simply notice that it's arising and let it go.

The ability to regulate and manage our attention is one of the most important skills needed in working with the self, which will be discussed further in chapter 7. It is the core practice of mindfulness. With training, we can decide what we put our attention on. As leaders, learning this transformational skill should be a priority.

WHY DO WE NEED TO PAY ATTENTION?

The short answer is that learning to pay attention allows us to make the best decisions based on present facts from a deep place of compassion and wisdom. If we focus on the past, we make decisions based on regret. If we focus on the future, we make decisions based on fear and anxiety. In both cases, decisions are not grounded alongside objective, present reality. Company X nearly took action on things that hadn't even happened yet. Once they stopped circling the dot in fear, they started relating from openness and curiosity, which allowed them to see all the possibilities for effective action.

The bigger why is this: when we focus on the past (and experience regret) or the future (and experience anxiety), we get stuck in a mental rut:

- Focusing on the past or future leads to a compulsive thought cycle, which ultimately gives rise to suffering.
- Our suffering then creates the deep desire to either avoid or hang on to certain things.
- Our choices are then limited to those born out of aversion (avoidance) or attachment (holding on). We aren't free to see all of the possible options.
- Ultimately, being stuck in reactivity and acting from this consciousness causes more suffering (depression, anxiety, stress), which then affects decision-making, decreases productivity, and limits innovation.

Let's look at the different aspects of this pattern and explore how learning to pay attention can set us free to be more effective leaders.

COMPULSIVE THOUGHT CYCLE

The mind's natural propensity is to stay in the past or in the future. Past, future, past, future, past, future. The untrained mind jumps back and forth compulsively. We might find ourselves obsessing over a past failure at work, then worrying how that will play out when promotion time rolls around, then wishing we hadn't made the mistake, and on and on. This compulsive thought cycle keeps us trapped in the Fear Zone. Our context, or the way we're relating, is firmly entrenched in fear, not trust.

When we're compulsively ruminating on the past or future, we're not grounded in what's happening right now. As a result, we can't see the wisest action given the current reality.

REACTIVITY

Throughout our day, we contact, or interact with, things in the external world through our five senses: sight, sound, smell, taste, touch. As I mentioned earlier, we also contact our thoughts. When we make contact, we initially react in one of three ways: we find the thing pleasant, unpleasant, or neutral. Reactivity in this sense is completely normal. It is part of our evolutionary neurobiological wiring. There's nothing we can do about reactivity arising, so we don't need to worry when it does so.

We become stuck, however, when we become caught up in the pleasant–unpleasant cycle. For example, I eat my first handful of potato chips (my favorite being salt and vinegar), and the taste is very pleasant. I want to experience more of that pleasant feeling, so I take another handful of chips, then another and another until the entire bag is gone!

Then, I feel unpleasant. "Oh no, my beloved salt and vinegar chips have disappeared!" I mourn. Now I need to get rid of this unpleasant feeling. I must get more of this wonderfully tasty, deep-fried, and misleadingly marketed healthy snack. I will not be happy until I remove this unpleasant feeling.

And so it goes, around and around. Pleasant, hold on to the feeling; unpleasant, remove the feeling. This cycle is at the root of fear. We become attached at either end—attached to keeping the feeling going or attached to relieving it. We are not in present reality.

The same thing happens when we come in contact with a thought. If we have a thought we don't like, we try to make it go away. If we have a thought we like, we try to make it stay. These are two sides of the same reactivity coin, both based on fear.

As mentioned in chapter 1, thoughts are not reality. They do not reflect what is happening in the external world. The fact that a thought arises doesn't make the thought true. When we're stuck in a compulsive thought cycle, however, we start reacting to our thoughts as if they represent reality.

If we're not paying attention, we won't realize we're reacting to our thoughts this way. We will continue making choices in the external (real) world based on our internal (not-reality) thoughts and feelings. If we can't see that we're stuck in reactivity, then we can't get out of our stuckness. This is why paying attention is so important. When we understand that we're having a reaction, we have choices. Let's say I'm driving down the street and stop at a red light. I hear loud, thumping bass emanating from the car next to me, and I react: that's pleasant, unpleasant, or neutral. How I *respond* next depends on whether I'm paying attention.

When I am not paying attention to how I'm relating, my choices are limited. Unconsciously, I get hooked into my reaction and can only respond in one of two ways: make it stay or get rid of it. If my initial reaction is "That's pleasant," I desperately try to make the music stay. The need to have it continue becomes a craving. I have a fear of losing that pleasant sound, and I will do anything to keep it around. I might take out my phone and compulsively search for my own thumping music. On the other hand, if my initial reaction is "That's unpleasant," I'll do whatever it takes to make the music go away, and fast. I need to avoid it. I have a fear of having to endure that sound one second longer. In my agitation, I might flip off the other driver or give him a dirty look. Either way, if I'm in fear, I only have one choice after my initial reaction. My well-being is challenged, and I need to do something to fix it. Now!

On the other hand, if I'm paying attention to my first unbidden reaction, I can see that I have many options.

For example, if I recognize I don't like the music, I can raise my window or turn up my own radio. I can ask the person if he would be willing to turn down the volume. Or I can just listen to the music, knowing that the light is going to change any second and I can drive away. Something in my conditioning doesn't like the music, but I'm not a slave to my conditioning. I don't have to move away from the music, unless that seems like the wisest choice. I also don't have to criticize or judge the guy playing the music, and I don't have to judge my experience of the music as right or wrong. It just is what it is. I can choose not to suffer regardless of what the music is doing. I can be with the music and my experience of it.

People have been convinced that mindfulness means they won't have a reaction to things. This is incorrect. Reactivity happens; it's a natural, normal occurrence, and there's nothing we can do about it. Our likes and dislikes have been conditioned into us by upbringing, environment, and so on. If I'm not paying attention, however, I can get hooked into my natural, unbidden reactivity and go from "I don't like that music" to "That guy is stupid. Why is he playing that music? I just want it to stop!" Conversely, I can go from "I really like that music" to "I want more of that music. I really don't want it to stop. I have to find a way to listen to that music every day and if I don't, I just won't be happy. Ever!" Either way, I've fallen into reactivity, and I'm not free to choose a wise and compassionate response.

When I was moving up the corporate ladder in my thirties, I had not awakened to the idea of paying attention to how I was relating. As I received promotions and added letters behind my name, I also received accolades from those around me. My initial, immediate reaction to the attention was "I like this." I set out to accumulate more certificates and degrees because I wanted to continue receiving praise and to look good. More than that, I was afraid of losing the sense of accomplishment and attention. I became trapped in my need to keep achieving. I couldn't stop, even when my relationship was eroding, I had gained fifteen pounds, and I had nightly panic attacks.

Is a promotion or advanced degree a problem in itself? Not at all. But if I'm pursuing them out of fear of losing the accolades, what happens if I'm passed over for a promotion? I'm devastated. My whole identity is threatened. (Spoiler: more on our relationship with our identity in chapter 7.)

In any of these scenarios, the thing itself is not the issue. It's how I'm relating to it. If I'm not paying attention, however, I forget this truth and I begin to think the external phenomenon is the problem, and then I start reacting to the thoughts and sensations that come along with the initial reaction to the phenomenon.

When we're stuck in reactivity, we make decisions that

are not based on present reality. If I'm a leader, those decisions will most likely impact the well-being of those I'm leading. As leaders, we are not isolated entities. We're connected with others. We're dealing with other people's hopes, dreams, and aspirations.

When we're not present, we start believing our fear-based stories, or internal explanations for external phenomena:

- I need to work a lot harder, or I'll lose my job.
- My boss's door is closed again. That means something bad is going to happen.
- My door is closed again. What will my team think? They'll think I'm unavailable. They'll think I'm a bad leader.

Then we make decisions based on these stories. For example, to avoid the perception that we are unavailable, we might leave our door open all the time, and as a result our work output drops.

NEW PATHWAYS FOR RESPONSE

When we're stuck in the fear and reactivity loop, our actions become repetitive. We can't move forward in our lives, even though the current pattern is causing suffering for ourselves and those around us. By learning to pay attention, we break the cycle and open new pathways for response.

One new pathway is empathy and compassion. When we're stuck in reactivity, we don't have access to these responses. Fear drives us to be self-centered, selfish, and narrow because our well-being feels threatened. If I believe I'm in danger of losing my job or that losing a business contract means I'm a failure as a person, I'll do whatever it takes to prevent that from happening. My decisions regarding direct reports will spring from this limited, selfish, unempathetic, and uncompassionate place. However, if I can unhook myself from reacting to a perceived experience of threat, I am free to access empathy and compassion for others. My decisions will then flow from a place of wisdom instead of self-indulgence.

Some people have a skewed view of compassion and think it means letting people walk all over them or avoiding hurt feelings. That's not compassion. Healthy compassion involves saying yes and no. If one of my team members is unhappy at the company and has struggled for months in his role, it might be time to fire him. If I'm stuck in fear, however, I might avoid firing him because I don't want to upset the person. I might even think this action (or lack thereof) shows compassion. In truth, it doesn't. I don't want to deal with the person's reaction, so I choose comfort instead of what's best for the employee and the company. When we're stuck in reactivity, we don't have access to this healthy yes and healthy no.

LESS SUFFERING AND MORE PRODUCTIVITY

Research shows that the recycling of thoughts, or rumination, is linked to both depression and anxiety.[2] Research also shows that mindfulness practices like paying attention and noticing one's real-time experience can decrease our experience of depression and anxiety. When we don't spend our energy ruminating on the past and future, we start to relax and depressive symptoms become less severe.

Psychologist Richard J. Davidson studied 1,258 patients who participated in mindfulness-based approaches as part of their clinical intervention to combat depression. He found that approaches such as awareness meditation and body scan meditation reduced the risk of depressive relapse within a sixty-week follow-up period. He also found that mindfulness-based cognitive therapy was most effective for patients who experienced more severe depression before treatment.[3]

People who know how to pay attention report having greater levels of well-being. They experience less depression, anxiety, and stress.[4] They are more present in their lives. It stands to reason that leaders who pay attention on the transformational plane exhibit more skillful actions on the transactional plane.

When whole teams learn to pay attention with mindfulness, they enjoy greater creativity, innovation, and problem-solving. Think of the Company X team I worked with regarding the Glassdoor posting. As soon as they stopped ruminating about the future and focused on the facts in front of them, they came up with a multistep action plan. The team had burned at least twelve hours stuck in reactivity of thought, circling the issue but producing no action. Once they came back to paying attention, they had a solution in minutes and their stress disappeared. They saved time, money, and energy. They experienced improved well-being. A veritable bonanza of benefits and freedom.

SCIENCE SUPPORTS THE PRACTICE

When the concepts and practices of mindfulness and meditation first made it to the West not so long ago, they didn't contain much supporting scientific evidence. They came from the contemplative approaches to living found in the Eastern traditions of Buddhism. At the time of the Buddha, these approaches were not named Buddhism, just as Christian practices were not named Christianity at the time of Jesus. Those names came much later as people attempted to categorize their core teachings. The same thing occurs within the world of philosophy, with some philosophers being classified as stoics or existentialists, many of whom would not have labeled themselves as such. Getting caught up in naming conventions stops many from learning through these wise practices.

Nevertheless, due to the progression of technology and neuroscience, much more research has become available to say that yes, in fact, meditation and mindfulness practices do work not only to change the way the brain functions but also to support us in living more beneficial lives. I will explore a couple of the current and most beneficial articles here.

As humans, we are naturally wired with a negativity bias. Paul Rozin and his colleagues at the University of Pennsylvania proposed that the negative events of our lives carry greater weight on our psychological bandwidth than pleasant experiences.[5] Therefore, not only do we remember the negative events more reliably, but we can also be prone to allowing the positive ones to slide right off of us. "We are Teflon for the good and Velcro for the bad," says neuropsychologist Dr. Rick Hanson.[6] This negative wiring helps explain why we ruminate often about all of the bad things that can go wrong. Even when life is moving along swimmingly, we can suddenly find ourselves considering how the other shoe is going to drop any second! The negative events of our lives simply stick with us more easily, and the mind wanders in that direction, attempting to predict what will keep us safe. Mindfulness can help us work with this innate wiring.

Psychologists Matthew A. Killingsworth and Daniel T. Gilbert provide one of the most compelling articles on what happens when we let our minds wander between past and future. They used an app to gather information about how people were feeling at different points in the day. This approach is known as experience sampling and is intended to capture a person's real-time experience. Killingsworth and Gilbert contacted more than 2,250 volunteers and garnered over 250,000 data points on subjects' thoughts, feelings, and behaviors as they went about their lives.[7]

The results were telling. People spent 46.9 percent of their time thinking about something other than what they were actually doing. Additionally, people were less happy when their minds were wandering. Moreover, it was the amount of mind wandering that correlated to the level of unhappiness, not the present activity. This is a very powerful distinction. People's activity was not the cause of their happiness or unhappiness in the moment. How present they were to the activity mattered much more than the activity itself.

Even when people were thinking about pleasant topics,

they still reported being less happy than when they were present with their actual activity. Of course, when thinking about neutral or unpleasant topics, they were even less happy. Our ability to give our attention fully to what is happening or what we are experiencing in the moment is a relevant contributor to our happiness in the moment. This study also provides greater understanding into one of the pitfalls of goal setting and striving to achieve, which we will explore in further chapters.

Are there times when meditation practices may not be beneficial? Perhaps. Dr. Willoughby Britton and Dr. Jared Lindahl from Brown University have interviewed people who practiced meditation and subsequently experienced difficulties. For example, upon meditating and coming in contact with their thoughts during a retreat, some individuals freaked out. They became overwhelmed at what they found when they were still and present, and they couldn't control these newly surfacing thoughts. In addition, after returning home from a retreat, some people found they had increased anxiety and more difficulty concentrating on everyday tasks. In the Buddhist tradition, these difficulties are known as hindrances to meditation.[8]

HINDRANCES TO MEDITATION

If you decide to try meditation and find yourself experiencing difficulties, you're not alone. Here are some of the most common hindrances people encounter when they start a meditation practice:

- *Restlessness.* Restlessness can show up mentally as worry or anxiety and physically as the inability to be still.
- *Sleepiness.* Some people find they fall asleep when they try to meditate.
- *Desire.* Mediation can bring about an enjoyable sense of calm and relaxation, which is great, but people can become attached to that experience and try to make it stay.
- *Aversion.* Conversely, meditation can bring up bad thoughts and feelings, and people can react by trying to make them go away.
- *Doubt.* Many people doubt meditation will bring peace or alleviate their suffering.

For more information on meditation in general, hindrances in particular, and the antidote for these hindrances, go to www.insight-meditationcenter.org.

Drs. Britton and Lindahl also found that certain factors at the practitioner level can influence a person's meditation experience. For example, someone with a history of personal trauma or unresolved psychological issues might not find the peace they seek through meditation alone. They might find it nearly impossible to sit still and be with their thoughts. In addition, a practitioner's experience can be impacted by his or her relationships. For example, someone going through a divorce may be too agitated to meditate at times. Additionally, it may be such that certain types of meditation (e.g., body scan versus loving-kindness) are better suited for different types of individuals at different times.[9]

Science shows us that much of our stress results from our innate wiring, and so our reactivity isn't our fault. Of course, this doesn't mean we don't take responsibility. The good news is that even though the root cause is beyond our control, we can still engage in practices that help us manage our experience. As with many new skills, however, we must consistently bring meditation and mindfulness into our daily lives. This requires practice and consistent effort. We are creatures of habit, which is both beneficial and not so beneficial, as we have seen. Without consistently working with our awareness, we simply habituate back to our innate negativity bias and wandering mind.

If you want to enjoy well-being and productivity as a leader and help your team enjoy the same, you must train your attention first. The next chapter shows you how.

EXERCISE: WORKING WITH ATTENTION

Goal: Paying attention is a central transformational skill. This exercise will introduce you to the practice of consciously shifting your attention—that is, choosing where to put your attention.

Process: Look around the room and pick a neutral object, something that doesn't hold much meaning, for example, a doorknob or lamp. Place your attention on that object. Notice you can consciously direct your focus to the object.

Next, move your attention from the object to your body. Choose an area that doesn't carry much attachment or meaning for you. Notice whether you feel a sensation in that body part. Choose a different area of your body, and direct your attention to that spot. Notice how you can literally put your focus where you want it; keeping it there is a different story. We'll explore how to do that in the next chapter.

CHAPTER 3

PAYING ATTENTION, PART TWO

HOW TO TRAIN THE ATTENTION

"Only that day dawns to which we are awake."

—HENRY DAVID THOREAU, *WALDEN*

If you participated in the exercise at the end of chapter 2, you practiced paying attention. Now we're going to take that skill a step further.

First, consider the fact that as you sit there reading this chapter, you're breathing. That's really great news. Even better, it's happening without you consciously doing anything. You would think that since we breathe all day every day, we would notice it happening, but typically, we do not. For most of us, breathing is a neutral experience. Pause for a second and simply notice the fact that you are breathing.

Next, notice that in the act of reading, you're using your sense of sight to see words on the page. Notice that sight is happening when you look at the book or the coffee cup on the table or the clock on the wall.

Notice that as you are using your eyes to read, you are also able to hear noises. What sounds are occurring around you? Also notice that hearing itself is happening.

Finally, notice that thoughts arise unbidden as you read this book. They simply happen. Some thoughts relate to what you're reading ("This is the best book I've ever read!") and others concern something completely unrelated ("I wish that dog would stop barking.").

Training the attention involves learning to consciously shift our focus between many different phenomena, external and internal. We can learn to pay attention to breath, sight, hearing, sensations, and thoughts. This is a small glimpse of what it means to intentionally bring your awareness to what's happening in the present moment. This is a key practice and one that supports us in discovering our greatest well-being.

Psychologist Dr. Brad Blanton, author of *Radical Honesty: How to Transform Your Life by Telling the Truth*, points out that there are three specific areas we can place our attention. He calls these inside, outside, and upside-down. We can put our attention on what is occurring *inside*, or with the sensations in our bodies, our senses, and our general reaction (pleasant, unpleasant, and neutral). We can also put our attention on the *outside*, that is, what is occurring in the environment itself: where we are sitting or the people in the room. Lastly, we can put our attention on our thoughts, or the *upside-down* part of our experience—upside-down because most of our thoughts aren't true or grounded in reality.[1] In addition to Blanton's three, we can also place our attention on our mind states (how we are relating to an experience) as well as the experience itself; that is, all that we are aware of at any given time, both within and without. This is the essence of this section of the book.

According to Jack Kornfield and the Buddhist perspective, there are four foundations of mindfulness:

1. Contemplation of the body: to see that the body is not itself a unified thing but is instead a collection of different parts, like a car. If we remove all of the parts of a car and lay them on the ground, is it still a car? Like many other entities, the body comes into existence for a time and passes away. At the root, contemplation

of the body is the consideration of how I am relating identity-wise to this thing called a body.

2. Contemplation of feelings: to be aware of the root of feeling as pleasant, unpleasant, or neutral. As well, we see that each feeling arises and passes away and is not "my" feeling. When we see a feeling as a sensation or a set of sensations, we begin to see the selfless (not attached to the self) nature of feelings themselves. No one owns the market on anger (although we certainly like to think it's everyone but us).

3. Contemplation of thoughts: to be aware of the arising nature of thoughts and see that they exist only in reaction to phenomena as we come in contact with them. Different thoughts arise unbidden, dependent on causes and conditions. We see that, in truth, we are not our thoughts.

4. Contemplation of mind states and their relation to experience itself: to "come and see." In particular, we become aware of those moments when the mind is attached to an experience or averse to it. In my experience, the mind states of hate (aversion), greed (attachment), and delusion (autopilot) are at the root of our suffering. We consider our entire experience as something occurring *inside of* ourselves instead of something happening *out there*. We see that as we interact with the world around us, we are reacting to all things: our senses, our thoughts, and all things that happen in between, such as our attachments, aver-

sions, and the releasing of them. As we come and see, we are aware of how things truly are. It is here that we begin to see the truth of impermanence in all things.[2]

Training the attention is not easy, and yet being mindful is simple. It's a transformational skill that requires consistency and cultivation. In this chapter we'll discuss how to train the attention by:

- developing a daily practice of meditation
- learning to identify when we're running on autopilot
- practicing mindfulness everywhere
- learning to regulate the "beam" of our attention
- developing a practice of gratitude

The chapter ends with a body scan meditation to help you practice and develop your new skills.

PRACTICE MEDITATION AND DAILY MINDFULNESS

As mentioned in chapter 2, mindfulness can be defined as "paying attention in a particular way, on purpose, in the present moment and nonjudgmentally."[3] Meditation is the formal practice used to pay attention, develop concentration, and learn to recognize our present experience. Formal meditation trains us to become more mindful. It's possible to rest without sleeping, but if you never sleep, you won't be getting the most effective rest. The same is true of meditation and mindfulness: it is possible to incorporate mindfulness practices without formally meditating, but if you don't meditate, you may not be as effective with your mindfulness practices.

Studies show that formal meditation has a great impact on our mental and physical well-being. Equally important, however, is bringing mindfulness practices into daily life. It's one thing to go away on a retreat, where it's quiet and the kids aren't clamoring and the boss isn't calling. It's another thing to bring mindfulness into everyday living with its many distractions. All the more reason for us to practice daily in training our ability to pay attention. We need to learn to be with our experience without fighting against it, trying to hang on to it, or trying to make it something it isn't.

RETURN TO THE BREATH

We begin our mindfulness practice with meditation. We can start by simply focusing on the breath. We use the breath as an anchor, as it is fairly reliable.

Try this: sit quietly where you are. Turn your attention to your breathing and keep it there. Soon, you'll realize you're no longer paying attention to your breath. Instead you're focused on the smell of jasmine or the sound of a lawnmower or the thought that your in-laws are coming to visit next week. This is completely normal. In the process of focusing on your breathing, you still come into contact with your environment through your senses and thoughts, and you still have unbidden reactions to those phenomena as well. The great news is that we don't need to worry about it.

As soon as you realize you're distracted, gently bring your attention back to breathing by asking yourself two questions:

1. What's happening now?
2. How am I relating?

The first question brings the attention to the present, to what is happening right now. It brings us to the first moment of waking up to what is actually occurring. In this case, we were focusing on the breath and we suddenly found our attention had fixated on something else.

The second question helps you identify whether you're relating from fear or trust. In essence, it's the same question God asked Adam and Eve in Genesis 3. After their misstep in the garden, Adam and Eve were afraid and attempted to hide. Then God called out, "Where are you?" This is the key question to ask ourselves as we consider where we are relating to all things in life. Are you on the dot, repeating and recycling suffering from fear? Or have you stepped off of the dot?

Even during this simple breathing exercise, you might get stuck in reactivity and fear. If you remember your in-laws are coming and then remember a stressful incident from the last time they visited, you might start worrying about their upcoming stay and shift into a compulsive thought cycle. Or you might notice that your knee is aching and begin to wonder why it's aching and whether this is something bad like your friend had when he tore his cartilage. Asking yourself, "How am I relating?" can help you acknowledge you may be wanting to stop or hold onto something out of fear. After you become aware, you can shift your attention back to the breath. You will do this again and again.

Here's an example of how this might play out: I'm sitting with my eyes closed and focusing on my breath. Suddenly, I notice a leaf blower in the background. I think, "Oh, there's that leaf blower guy again! I wish that noise would go away." Then I realize I'm no longer resting my attention on my breathing. I ask myself, "What's happening now?" I'm thinking about the leaf blower. Then I ask, "How am I relating to that sound?" I don't like it. Then I tell myself, "Return to the breath." A half breath later, I realize I want a cigarette. But I don't even smoke! Then I ask, "What's happening now?" I'm thinking I wish I felt more relaxed. Then I ask, "How am I relating to that thought?" I wish my brain would stop. Then I remind myself to return to the breath. Every time I become aware that my attention has drifted away from the breath, I simply and gently return my attention to watching it come and go.

This exercise also illustrates how easily we fall into reactivity. We're focusing on our breathing, then suddenly we're off thinking about tomorrow's big meeting with the boss. That's typically where the mind goes: to the future or the past. Alternatively, we might feel a body sensation like pain in our knee, and then we fall into aversion and thinking about how we wish it would stop hurting.

If we realize our attention has shifted away from our breathing and is now focused on wishing reality were different than it is, we can acknowledge that. We can welcome the reality that we're resisting this moment in life as it is. The goal is to train the attention to fully comprehend what is happening in our lives at any given moment. That includes *all* present thoughts, feelings, and sensations, as well as the way we are relating to all of these incredible phenomena. We want to become fully aware of how we're relating each moment because our experience in life is created by the way we are relating.

When we fully comprehend what is happening, we can then, and only then, start to take responsibility. We stop blaming the external and start owning that our experiences with people, objects, sensations, and events are all based on how we're relating to those things, not the things themselves. How I'm relating to those things determines how much joy, peace, love, and equanimity I experience in each moment. My well-being is completely within my power and control, despite the reality that life itself is not.

It is very difficult to become skilled at meditation without some form of consistent practice. When people ask me if meditation works, I like to explain that it works just like a lock on a door. All locks have one inherent design flaw: you must turn the key to get them to work! Being mindful and training the attention take regular practice. That said, meditation alone isn't going to bring you ultimate peace or make you an empathetic, effective leader, although it is foundational to doing so. As they say in yoga circles, you have to bring it off the mat. We have to bring mindfulness into daily life.

FLY THE PLANE YOURSELF

Dr. Jon Kabat-Zinn once said that no person has actually been in the shower.[4] In other words, when we're in the shower, we're often not really present. We've taken so many showers that we switch to autopilot and get caught up in our neutral same-old, same-old experience. Our bodies stand under the water, but our minds do not pay attention to what the water feels like or what we're actually doing.

As mentioned, our reaction to what we encounter is pleasant, unpleasant, or neutral. When we have neutral experiences, we more readily switch to autopilot and going through the motions. Practicing mindfulness enables us to recognize when we're on autopilot.

One afternoon a friend and I decided to walk over to the local coffee shop for one of our favorite drinks (an almond milk latte, in case you were wondering). It was a truly beautiful sunny spring day, and we commented on the lovely weather. I could hear birds singing, and there was a slight breeze on my face as the sun warmed my shoulders. We arrived at the coffee shop around lunchtime and took our place in line behind the many others who wanted to buy their favorite coffee drink. A few minutes after standing in line, my friend suddenly said, "What is taking so long? Do they only have one person taking orders?" I smiled and asked her if there was somewhere she had to get to right away. Of course, she didn't. I knew that we had nothing else to be doing at the moment but getting our coffee. Her experience had quickly shifted from pleasant to neutral to unpleasant.

When you become fully present to each moment, you will never again "wait" in line. When you experience waiting, you have left your present experience and moved into the future ("When am I going to get my coffee?"). Like standing in the shower, waiting in line can feel like a boring, mundane moment in life, and we tend to not give these moments our attention. As a result, we slip into autopilot. To fly the plane and stay off autopilot, we need to be aware of our reaction to neutral experiences as well as the pleasant and unpleasant ones. We need to consciously bring our attention back to the present when our minds wander while doing the boring, mundane stuff of life.

When we wake up to our experience each moment, life becomes richer. We find a new appreciation for the seemingly mundane, or neutral, moments of our days, like "waiting" in line for coffee. As the Killingsworth study revealed, we find greater enjoyment in any activity when we are fully present to what we are doing. Paying attention also helps us reduce the automatic pattern of reacting out of fear. We see what's happening more quickly, and we can stop, notice, and shift our attention. We can make conscious, intentional choices about our behavior.

REGULATE THE BEAM

Our attention is like the beam from a flashlight. It can be regulated to focus on a narrow or broad area. Using a narrow beam allows us to see a small area in great detail. Widening the beam allows us to see the totality of what's in front of us.

For example, we can shift our attention from "What about me?" to "What about you or us?" We can give our full attention to a document we're writing or a conversation we're having and keep all distractions in the background. Attention is a gift we can use to work for us to benefit all beings everywhere.

However, when we fail to regulate the beam—when we let our attention drag us around by the nose—our lives tend to feel much less cohesive, fun, and relaxing. We begin to behave just like our untrained mind. We run from this thing to that and don't even notice that we left this behind and forgot all about that.

Being able to regulate our attention, switching back and forth as needed, is a very helpful skill to navigate our work and our lives.

BE MINDFUL EVERYWHERE

When we are present, we have insight into what is actually happening and what is possible. We are no longer stuck in automatic reactions of thinking, feeling, and behaving. We can do everything with awareness. We can engage in mindful walking, mindful eating, mindful listening, mindful swimming—anything.

Engaging in these everyday activities from a place of

mindfulness is another way to train the attention and practice focusing awareness on the present. When you set out on a walk, for example, focus on the act of walking. Realize that you are walking. Notice the feeling of the ground under your shoes. Notice the pressure of your shoes against your feet with each step. What you'll probably notice is that as you're walking, your attention wanders. Suddenly, you'll realize you're no longer focusing on your steps. You're thinking about how warm the sun is, or you're trying to find the bird that's chirping. When this happens, pause and ask yourself, "What's happening?" Notice whether judgment has arisen. Ask yourself how you're relating. Bring your attention back to your steps.

Mindfulness and the gift of waking up isn't reserved for the chosen few who run away to the Himalayas, although you might like to do that. Anyone can become mindful and skilled at paying attention—if they practice intentional thoughts and actions in everyday situations.

There's also a very important difference between mindfulness and self-consciousness. Mindfulness is being aware of what's happening around and inside you at any given moment. This is different from believing you have to think through every step of every activity with concern about getting it right. The distinction is the level of concern, worry, and constant evaluation of your self-worth and effectiveness in life. That is not mindfulness.

THE BEGINNING OF FREEDOM

Many people come to mindfulness practices because they are suffering, me included. There's certainly nothing wrong with that. However, the goal of mindfulness (if there is one) is not to change what we are experiencing. The goal is to be with the totality of our experience without reacting from fear, not even fear of our reactivity. In other words, without pushing the experience away, ignoring it, or trying to hang on to it. When we can do that, we are truly free to act. We can step off the dot and into new possibilities. This is where our greatest wisdom abides.

When we are truly free to act, we are not swayed by either-or thinking, feeling, and acting. This enables us to innovate and create solutions that are much more aligned with the well-being of everyone, instead of just our own. In addition, freedom gives us the ability to see that most of our suffering is created by the desire for permanence and predictability.

In chapter 4, we will focus specifically on thoughts and emotions, two parts of our experience that many of us need to learn to work with, instead of against.

EXERCISE: BODY SCAN MEDITATION

Goal: Through this exercise, you'll learn how to recognize and experience physical sensation. Think of a radio. Just as you would dial in to listen to a certain channel, you can dial in your attention to different sensations: breathing, tasting, hearing, and so on. In this exercise, you're going to tune your attention to the physical sensations in different areas of your body.

Set-Up: You may do this meditation in any posture that allows you to feel relaxed and alert: sitting, lying, or standing. I also recommend experimenting with different postures at different times when you do the body scan meditation.

You may also close your eyes or leave your eyes partially open, with your gaze a few feet in front of you. You may experiment with either approach, but choose one and don't switch in the middle of your practice session. Allow the body to relax as much as it is available to do so without forcing anything. Take a few deep inhales (and, of course, exhales), and relax.

Process: Gently bring your attention to the breath. Simply rest your attention there for a period of several minutes, allowing the attention to become steady. After a couple of minutes, bring your attention to a palm-sized area on the top of your head. Continue focusing on a palm-sized area as you scan down the head, face, neck, and so forth, systematically noticing different sensations occurring in and on the body.

After you pass the front and back of the neck, move to the right shoulder and scan down the right arm, then move to the left shoulder and arm. Scan your chest, abdomen, and back, and then scan each leg. After scanning the feet, begin moving back up the body, scanning all the way to the top of the head.

As you scan, simply notice sensation. You may become aware that certain parts of the body ache and want your attention. You may also notice your mind wanders. If you become too distracted by thoughts, simply return to the breath for a few seconds and then return to the scanning. Whatever you notice, dial in your attention to that sensation. As best you can, notice fully and completely, without judgment.

Move through this exercise at your own pace and in a way that allows you to fully notice sensation within a palm-sized space. It's not a race, and there's no right scanning speed. The goal is to focus your attention on the sensations you feel, however long that takes, while continuing to scan the body up and down.

If you would like to listen to a guided meditation of this body scan, please go to www.wakingupaleader.com.

CHAPTER 4

WORKING WITH THOUGHTS AND EMOTIONS

"Pleasure and displeasure feel qualitatively different. You and I might not agree that a specific object or event produces pleasure or displeasure—I find walnuts delicious whereas my husband calls them an offense against nature—but each of us can, in principle, distinguish one from the other. These feelings are universal, even as emotions like happiness and anger are not, and they flow like a current through every waking moment of your life."

—LISA FELDMAN BARRETT, *HOW EMOTIONS ARE MADE*

After working on a big project for several months, Steve submitted a stack of paperwork, expecting feedback and a dash of praise for his hard work. The next day, his boss sent an email: "Looks great. Let's keep moving forward."

"Looks great? That's all?! What does that mean?" Steve thought. He felt the email lacked substance and any hint of appreciation. He also worried that his boss wasn't that impressed. "Now I won't get that promotion."

Steve stewed on these events for a week before I talked to him. After Steve relayed the story, I asked him for the facts. Then I asked what he was feeling.

"I'm angry. I feel really annoyed. He always does this! He never appreciates the work I put in," Steve replied.

Steve was stuck in reactivity. He added meaning to his boss's email ("He never appreciates the work I put in") and reacted to that story as if it were true. His emotions kicked in, and he couldn't break free of the cognitive-emotional loop.

To help Steve see this, we first broke down fact versus story: what a video recorder would have captured versus his interpretation.

Then I asked him, "How is this familiar? You're feeling undervalued, not appreciated, right? Where else have you experienced that sense of trying to get ahead and not being recognized?"

After sharing a few examples he had experienced with

his wife, Steve said, "I guess I felt like that with my dad too. Like I could never do enough."

This was the root. Steve's response to the current situation with his boss followed a pattern that started with his dad. He was conditioned to see events and conversations through the lens of not feeling appreciated, and his brain was interpreting the current situation from the past.

After pointing out the pattern, I asked, "Is it possible that what you're telling yourself about not being appreciated isn't actually the truth in this instance?"

"Well, yeah, it's possible," Steve replied.

Next, Steve had to test his story. He had to approach his boss about the email and find out what he was really thinking.

At the meeting, Steve said, "Hey, I sent you the information for that project. Based on your brief response, I've been telling myself the story that you didn't appreciate the detail I put in. I also wondered if you even read what I sent."

"Absolutely not true," his boss replied. "I read the whole thing. The truth is that you work so well and do everything I ask so independently, I didn't feel like I had much to offer."

"Really?" Steve was dumbfounded.

"Yeah. You actually work at such a high level that I don't feel like feedback will help you much."

Steve had unconsciously trained his boss to see him as so independent that he didn't need the input. In doing so, he had inadvertently prevented his boss from seeing his vulnerabilities, areas where he actually did want help. Steve had become angry and blamed his boss for the lack of input, when Steve himself had just as much responsibility and created the scenario in which the boss was not giving him help.

This story illustrates the importance of waking up to the way we relate to thoughts and emotions. We can create our own misery because we act and interact based on stories fueled by emotion. The answer isn't to stuff or deny thoughts and emotions. The answer is to be aware and cultivate a healthy relationship with both.

PERCEPTION AND CONDITIONING

Emotion is a very real part of our experience as human beings. If we don't have a healthy relationship with our feelings, we'll live in fear of them, either fear that the bad ones will last forever or that the good ones won't last long enough. In addition, emotion drives our behavior and influences how we see the behaviors of others.

Our awareness of emotion is registered as a sensation, a feeling in the literal sense (a tingling or throbbing). For convenience, we label feelings so we can explain them to ourselves and others. The problem is that what I feel in my body and label *anger* may not be the same as what you feel in your body and label *anger*. There's no specific neurological pattern in the brain for anger, joy, or any other emotion. We aren't wired to interpret these experiences in the same way. We label feelings and sensations based on several factors, including our experience of the sensation as pleasant or unpleasant, conditioning, and past experience.

In addition, the sensations themselves may vary widely. While we definitely know something is pleasant versus unpleasant, we may not be able to say whether that pleasant feeling is joy or satisfaction. Two different people may use the same label to describe two different sensations. And the same sensation may be unpleasant in one context and pleasant or neutral in another.

For example, tingling in my toes is a sensation or feeling. My experience of that sensation will be pleasant, unpleasant, or neutral. This experience is largely determined by the threat appraisal my mind performs, which depends on the context. If I sit on the couch with my foot tucked under my leg, I might experience tingling in my toes. In this situation, I don't panic. Nothing bad is happening.

My foot has simply fallen asleep, so I move my foot and the tingling goes away.

However, if I'm sitting on the couch with both feet on the floor and my toes start tingling, I might think, "Why are my toes tingling? That's not supposed to be happening!" I perceive this feeling as threatening my well-being. Now this tingling is unpleasant. Same sensation, different context, and thus a different reaction.

We live in a world of perception. We witness a behavior, and then we categorize it. For example, if I see someone at work stomping down the hall, I might think, "Boy, she is really angry." I've thus assigned an emotion to her action based on my own perceptions and past conditioning. My workmate might not be feeling anger at all. Maybe her foot fell asleep and she was trying to wake it up.

This is exactly what happened to Steve in the chapter-opening story. Steve assigned an emotion to his boss based on his interpretation of what he read in the boss's email, then he reacted to the emotion he assigned. He made himself miserable over a perception that was nothing more than a series of thoughts.

Steve's story and the emotion he assigned to his boss came from his past conditioning with his dad. It's important to understand how conditioning affects our relationship with the stuff of life: what we come in contact with in the external world as well as our feelings and our thoughts.

CULTURAL CONDITIONING

We're taught to name and see colors in a certain way. Take blue, for example. We're taught what category constitutes blue and its different hues, what matches with it, and so on. Yet, you and I may still have different concepts of what is blue.

Scientifically speaking, blue lives at a certain wavelength: 450 nanometers. Three people could sit in front of that same 450-nanometer wavelength and experience it as three different colors. Someone from Papua New Guinea would experience that wavelength as what I have been told is green. At the same time, an American would experience it as blue because in that culture, a distinction is made between green and blue. Someone from Turkey would have yet another experience of the same wavelength: he would call it *lacivert*, or dark blue, because people from Turkey have a different category for blue.[1]

The wavelength hitting the eyes of all three people is exactly the same—450 nanometers—but they have three completely different experiences of that color because of the culturally influenced way they conceptualize that sensory information.

Likewise, each person's experience of emotion varies according to what they've been culturally conditioned to think about emotion. We categorize emotion as good or bad, as threatening or not, based on how we've been "trained" to view it. The truth is that emotions themselves are neutral. They are neither good nor bad, even though we may decide what is pleasant, unpleasant, or neutral and also judge others when these energies arise.

We all have different perceptions of what we are feeling based on what we've been taught and the environment in which we find ourselves. This conditioning leads us to make judgments about what emotions look like, which emotions are appropriate and acceptable given the situation, and how we're to handle emotions. As a child, you may have experienced the death of a pet. Perhaps this was the first time you experienced water spilling from your eyes. In response, a parent may have said, "Oh, you're feeling sad." Your conception of sadness has now been conditioned: water coming out of eyes equals sadness.

Perhaps your parent then said something like, "Stop crying. It's going to be okay." Now you've been taught something else about water coming out of your eyes: it's something to be stopped. You may have internalized this judgment as "Crying is not something I should do. It's bad."

As we grow up, we learn more about the experience of tears. For example, we learn that water coming out of our eyes when we're home alone watching *This Is Us* is not a problem. Water coming out of our eyes at the office, however, is. It's a problem because of the conditioning we've received telling us tears are okay in one situation and not in another.

LABELS AND JUDGING

In her book *How Emotions Are Made*, Lisa Feldman Barrett discusses the brain's role in creating our experience of emotion, turning the idea of external events being the "cause" of our experience inside out. As she explains, based on past conditioning, our brain predicts what emotions are appropriate given our current context. Alas, we also try to predict what others are thinking and feeling, or what they "should" be thinking and feeling. The problem is that we can't predict someone else's emotion based on their facial expression or actions. The only way to know for sure is to ask. Our often-erroneous labels can lead to faulty judgments and behavior.[2]

Consider this scenario: two people walk past each other in the hallway at the office. One person says hello to the other person as they pass. The other person doesn't respond at all. If we are watching this scene, we would expect the second person to return the hello. When they don't, we immediately attempt to figure out why. Our brain predicts that they "should" have responded. That seems like the normal response based on what we've been taught and conditioned to believe. When that doesn't occur, the brain has to resolve what just happened. Immediately, our brain acknowledges something is amiss and fills in the blanks to try to explain its faulty prediction. Subsequently, we may notice judgments (thoughts) quickly arising to make sense of it all.

We also judge ourselves based on emotional labels. Perhaps we've learned that women should not experience the emotion labeled *anger* and men should not be afraid or sad. What happens if I do experience anger as a woman? I react. I criticize myself for getting angry. I judge that experience as wrong, something to avoid. Then I want to get rid of that emotion and my unpleasant feeling associated with the experience, so I pretend it doesn't exist. But internally, I'm still reacting and, likely, experiencing anger, and this will affect my interactions with others.

Most of us have been taught two ways to deal with emotions: we pretend they don't exist, or we overreact to them. We're going to talk about a middle way: don't worry about them. When we experience the truth that thoughts and emotions are impermanent, we can learn to be with them instead of reacting to them or feeling as though there is something wrong with them, or us.

CULTIVATING A HEALTHY RELATIONSHIP WITH THOUGHTS AND EMOTIONS

James, vice president of a huge company, called me for coaching, but he didn't know what he wanted to talk about. I asked him some questions, and finally he said, "I just have this belief that no one can help me. Nothing is going to help me."

"If you can see the truth of that, you'll be a lot freer," I replied.

"What do you mean? If I see the truth that no one can help me?"

"No, if you actually see that statement for what it is. It's a thought that arises in your mind. It isn't real."

James was silent for about fifteen seconds. Then he started laughing.

"You're right," he said.

"You can decide how much attention you want to give that thought. You get to choose."

"So, I need to stop the thought."

"No, you can't stop the thought. That comes unbidden."

"But when I have that thought, it makes me feel a certain way."

"Thoughts and feelings work together. If you keep thinking 'nothing can help me, nothing can help me, I'm always going to stay the same,' then you're going to have a certain feeling. The body and mind work together."

At that moment, James had an epiphany: it's just a thought. He was thinking his thought was bothering him, but he was actually bothering his thoughts. Thoughts show up, and we hang on to them. If we would leave them alone, they would come and go like clouds in the sky.

As leaders like James with decision rights that affect others, we are wise to cultivate a healthy relationship with thoughts and emotions. If we don't, we become incapable of tapping into our greatest wisdom and compassion. We will take action based on fear-generated thoughts and on stories that aren't true, resulting in suffering for our team and ourselves. For example, if James were to continue believing his thought that nothing will help the situation, he might not reach out for support that his struggling team really needs. We need to change our mindset, challenge past conditioning, and learn how to pull ourselves out of the cognitive-emotional loop. This section provides those transformational skills.

WORKING WITH REACTIVITY

Contrary to what might seem to be true, we don't cause the feelings or sensations we label as emotions. Like thoughts, emotions just happen. We don't control the causes and conditions that produce the sensations.

That said, we are still responsible for the behaviors that spring from those emotions. The Greek stoic philosopher and former slave Epictetus spoke to this when he wrote, "We are disturbed not by what happens to us but by our thoughts about what happens."[3] When we believe our interpretations about what "shows up" in our lives and assert that we "know" the truth based on those interpretations, we see the beginnings of our reactive nature to the unpredictability of living.

Think of Steve from the chapter-opening story. He had certain thoughts, which generated certain emotions, which led him to view his boss in a certain way. He was responsible for any rude or inappropriate behavior that resulted from his subjective reality. Having a healthy relationship with our thoughts and emotions will enable us to maintain the best intentions and take the most skillful actions, as Steve was able to do once he became aware of what was happening for him. He took the courageous step of challenging his own story by talking to his boss directly.

In addition, if we want to learn true compassion and empathy, we must learn to be with our thoughts and emotions in a way that doesn't add a second arrow to our naturally occurring reactivity. When we react out of fear, we're only interested in making the experience stay or go away. We suffer, and we're not concerned with anyone else's feelings, ideas, or perspectives.

The ultimate truth of human experience is that nothing is permanent. Like everything else in life, thoughts and emotions come and go. In a sense, they aren't inherently real. They arise effortlessly and fade away in the same manner—if we leave them alone and accept them with compassion and understanding. The steps in cultivating a healthy relationship with thoughts and emotions revolve around this truth.

PAY ATTENTION

When Steve read his boss's email, he found it unpleasant. His identity felt threatened, and he felt the need to do something about it. His choices were limited and likely wouldn't create the highest levels of well-being for himself. He could storm out, stew about it for the week, gossip to his colleagues, yell at his boss, or quit. All of these actions would be aimed at getting rid of what Steve perceived as the problem: his boss. Life became either-or for Steve. He couldn't see any other options.

After I talked to Steve and helped him see that perhaps his thoughts weren't reality, he was open to seeing things differently. He started questioning some of his stories. He also realized his boss's email was simply words on the page. In a future incident like this, if he were paying attention, Steve could talk himself through the experience: "Okay, those are words on the page. I think my boss means this, but I shouldn't react as if he does because I'm not sure. I'm just going to acknowledge that I'm having an unpleasant feeling, but it will pass and I don't have to worry about it. Then I can see what wants to occur next and what the wisest action might be."

The first step to moving in a different direction is first realizing where we're at and then choosing the wisest path. This happens more readily if we've trained our attention and cultivated the daily practice of staying present and aware.

RETURN TO THE BREATH

We tend to believe all of our thoughts. We don't question them. We think something, so it must be true. William

James, considered to be the father of American psychology, said as much: "My experience is what I agree to tend to."[4]

Steve fell into this trap. He received the email from his boss on a Tuesday. I didn't talk to him until Friday. He believed his thoughts and lived in reactivity for four days.

When we finally spoke on the phone, I asked him, "Have you been upset all week?"

"Yeah," Steve said.

"Really? The whole week, every minute, you've been upset?"

"Well, no. Not every minute. I mean, I went to my kid's baseball game, and then I went out to dinner with my wife."

Because Steve and I had discussed these concepts before, he was able to see that he was creating his own experience. When he recycled the thoughts about the email from his boss, he was upset. But when he let it go, he was able to enjoy a baseball game and evening out with his wife. His experience wasn't permanent. It was constantly shifting.

When we get into a cognitive-emotional loop like Steve did, it's very difficult to think our way out of it. It's like we're trapped in a tornado of thoughts, emotions, and stories about the situation (figure 4.1). We can't distinguish reality from our interpretations, and we certainly can't see the "thing," or root belief, that's beneath the swirling thoughts and emotions. (For Steve, the thing was his relationship with his dad that he was now projecting onto his boss.) In a situation like this, the body scan meditation at the end of chapter 3 is quite beneficial. One of the ways to pull ourselves out of the cognitive-emotional loop is to come back to the body and the breath. The body is always in real time. The mind never is. The mind will go into the past and future. The body is always here in the present.

Figure 4.1. The fear-induced cognitive-emotional loop can feel like a tornado.

Neuroscience has shown that coming back to the body and focusing on our breathing calms down the sympathetic nervous system—our fight-or-flight response. It forces us to be present.

When I was on the phone with Steve, I used this technique to help him step out of the cognitive-emotional loop. I asked him, "What is actually happening in your body right now?"

"Just sensation," he said.

"Right. The stuff you're telling yourself in your head isn't actually here."

"No, it isn't."

"So, your boss doesn't hate you. You're not losing your job. You're not an underachiever."

"No. All that is here is sensation."

"And is there anything missing from this moment, right now?"

"No."

Coming back to the body is a way to get in touch with real-time sensation and out of the loop. Once we stop spinning, we come to a crossroads where we can see what is truly happening and then choose our next action (figure 4.2).

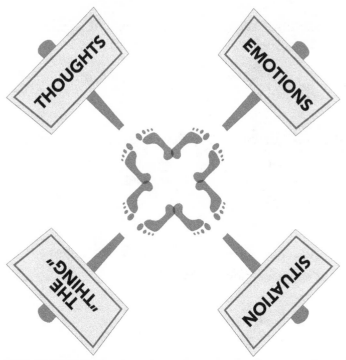

Figure 4.2 When we pull ourselves out of the swirling tornado, we can see each component of our experience for what it really is.

DISTINGUISH FACT FROM STORY

Another way to stop the cognitive-emotional loop is to do a fact-versus-story exercise. This concept has been written about in many different ways throughout the contemplative traditions, philosophy, and psychology. One of the more modern descriptions comes from psychologist Albert Ellis, who proposed the ABC Model in cognitive behavioral therapy.[5] The basic premise behind this model is that it isn't our events that cause our continued emotions and feelings; rather, it's our thoughts about those events. Any situation starts with an *activating* (A) event. I like to think of this as the thing that got my attention. Next, we have our *belief* (B) about that event. And lastly, we have the *consequence* (C) of those beliefs about that event. Ellis's ABC Model reinforces the wisdom seen in Epictetus and William James; that is, thoughts influence our experience.

The fact-versus-story exercise is a version of the ABC Model. First take out a sheet of paper and draw a line down the middle. On one side of the page write down the facts: the actions and words a video camera would record about the situation—words, sounds, actions. On the other side, write down the stories you're telling yourself about the events. You can do this for any situation where you feel threatened, where you feel yourself getting stuck in reactivity and fear. You might even choose one of the complaints from the inventory at the end of chapter 1.

In Steve's story, for example, there were only two facts:

1. Steve emailed his boss and attached the project to the email.
2. Steve's boss responded with the words, "Looks great. Let's keep moving forward."

Everything else was the story: feeling unappreciated, thinking he wouldn't get the promotion, fearing he might lose his job, and so on. These layered-on interpretations came out of the fact that Steve received an email and had an unpleasant experience. Then, he added a second arrow to the experience with his thoughts and interpretations. He had wanted something else to happen. When it didn't, he got scared and went into reactivity.

What often happens is that we add to the facts through our thoughts. We make up the meaning behind the words and actions recorded by the video camera. As discussed earlier, we then start reacting to these thoughts as if they represent reality.

Typically, the stories we make up come from reactivity and fear, if you've noticed. This is partly because of our innate negativity bias and the fact that the brain is a prediction machine. It makes predictions based on past experience, conditioning, and innate hardwiring.[6] The brain has a negativity bias in that it scans the environment for things that could go wrong, rather than what could go right, because it seems to be a good strategy to keep us safe. As a result, when something happens, our immediate *interpretation* of the facts is often negative and unnecessarily stress inducing.

Remember Company X from the beginning of chapter 2? They were stuck in a negativity bias and attempting to predict. They were ruminating about the future and predicting all the worst-case scenarios. Once they saw how they were relating, they came back to the facts and pulled themselves out of reactivity. As a result, they were free to innovate and figure out any and all solutions. But it started with distinguishing fact from story and returning their attention to the present facts. Notice that they didn't just tell themselves that they were making up a story and fly off on their magical unicorns. They came up with a couple of practical, wise actions to take. The key is that they did these things from presence and without the ensuing stress and drama that were getting entangled through their story.

CULTIVATE POSITIVE EMOTIONS

Humans have an innate desire to feel good and to have a life of well-being. The debate for the ages has been what this sense of well-being entails. Aristotle argued that well-being is more than a hedonic life of pleasure; that people want meaning and purpose, the ability to flourish, and fulfillment. He also believed that we find this well-being by living in line with our best virtues; that is, by being compassionate, helping others, and focusing on more than ourselves. Aristotle described living a life of the virtues as the "eudaimonic life."[7]

The science of positive psychology can help us understand how we might cultivate this life of well-being. As president of the American Psychological Association, Dr. Martin Seligman advocated for a positive psychology whose mission would be "to utilize quality scientific research and scholarship to reorient [psychological] science and practice toward human strength."[8] In other words, he suggested looking at the psychological impact of individuals' positive actions (human strengths) rather than focusing on eliminating the negative ones (human weaknesses, or the ways we cause suffering for ourselves). Positive psychology advocates for a balanced meliorism, adding good things to our lives as well as eliminating the harmful or unhealthy.

The question then becomes, what is positive? It differs for each person. Another way to think about "positive" is preferred versus nonpreferred. One person may prefer sunny days, New York-style pizza, and beachside walks. Another person may prefer a quiet moment in the country, thin-crust, and wild poolside dancing with her best friend. Doing these preferred actions brings positive emotions and improves one's sense of well-being.[9]

We can take actions that not only support us in living more mindfully but also enable us to intentionally practice those things in our daily lives that add to our ability (and that of others) to thrive. We can continue to cultivate our healthy mental state by incorporating practices of compassion, utilizing the best parts of ourselves (i.e., our strengths), and harnessing our naturally occurring resilience.

As mentioned, a negativity bias lives within each of us. We have a way of seeing the world wherein we try to predict all the things that could go wrong to make sure our well-being stays unthreatened and permanent. Positive emotion is a powerful antidote to this naturally occurring negativity. If we consciously cultivate positive emotional states, we can increase our well-being by counteracting the hardwired negativity bias.

When we do things that allow us to feel positive emotion such as joy and awe, we add to our overall well-being. There are many ways to cultivate positive emotions. Practice gratitude. Nurture experiences of awe by going to the Grand Canyon or looking at the ocean. Get a dog.

That said, if we're trying to use positive emotion to avoid our actual experience, then we're using positive emotion as an escape mechanism. Nonpreferred experiences are part of life. We will experience pleasure and pain, praise and blame. There's no way around it. Experiences will come, but they will also go. Embrace this truth, and you are on your way to a healthy relationship with thoughts and emotions.

EXERCISE: RAIN MEDITATION

Goal: This is an excellent meditation to use if you're really stuck in fear. This meditation was created by Michele McDonald, an insight meditation teacher.[10] The written guidelines follow, but the RAIN meditation is very powerful when someone else leads you through it. To hear the audio-guided meditation, go to www.wakingupaleader.com.

Setup: Sit in an upright, relaxed, and alert posture.

Process: Bring your attention to your breath. Allow the attention to settle on the breath. As you're resting your attention on the breath, begin to notice what is happening at this moment. You may notice thoughts are happening. You may notice feelings are happening. You may be aware of behaviors that are impacting you.

- **R**ecognition: The first step is to simply recognize you might be stuck. Pay attention to where you feel a little constricted in your body and mind. Maybe you notice a critical voice or that your breath is moving quickly. Simply notice what's going on at the moment. Become familiar with any experience and recognize it fully.

- **A**cceptance: The second step is to accept the experience you're having just as it is. As you recognize thoughts, emotions, and feelings, you might also notice body sensations. Allow them to be as they are without trying to fix or avoid them. You might notice that you're wishing certain things would stop. Maybe you wish you weren't having a certain thought or that you felt differently. You might feel fearful. Even as you notice these thoughts and feelings, allow them to be there. This is the path of letting an experience be, just as it is. Accept the reality of this moment, and gently allow yourself to open to what is happening now.

- **Investigation:** The third step is to investigate with a sense of curiosity, caring, and compassion with the experience. Ask yourself some questions about the things that have come to your attention: "What most wants attention right now? What am I believing? What stories am I telling myself?" If there's vulnerability present, ask yourself, "What does this vulnerable place want from me? What action is it pointing to?" It's important to approach this investigation with a nonjudgmental attitude. You're just asking yourself some questions, the way you would ask a friend.

- **Nonidentification:** The final step is nonidentification. Show yourself compassion. In that space of listening and trusting, in the nurturing part, give yourself some messages of reassurance. Then you will become less identified and see the truth of what's been happening. You will no longer be stuck in the trance of fear, judgment, and limiting beliefs. You will see the natural truth of your being.

PART II

THE FIVE
RELATIONSHIPS

Around the time I started waking up in my life, I began noticing what my coaching clients complained about. The most common topic: time. They complained about not having enough time. When they had too much time, they complained about being bored. The next most common topic was money. Clients never seemed to have enough money, and they stressed about having to work harder to make more. Then when they had enough, they worried about losing it.

One day as I listened to another stressed-out client, I realized, "Oh, my gosh. I complain about the same things!" I did a little internal survey and found my top complaint topics mirrored my clients'. In addition to time and money, we all worried about our sense of identity, our lack of true connection with others, and our fear of the unknown.

In Part II, we'll look at these five key relationships on two planes—the transformational and the transactional. We'll discuss the transformational skills from Part I and apply them in our relationships to time, money, the self, friendships, and the unknown. We'll also look at the transactional skills for interacting effectively, efficiently, and skillfully in the workplace.

We tend to get hooked in fear and reactivity around these five relationships, which creates suffering for ourselves and those around us, including those we lead. Learning to pay attention and live in the present in each area frees us to make wiser decisions, lead with compassion, and contribute to the well-being of others. In my experience, people who effectively manage these five relationships enjoy a higher level of well-being, personally and professionally.

CHAPTER 5

TIME

"This is the secret of life—to be completely engaged with what you are doing in the here and now. And instead of calling it work, realize it is play."

—ALAN WATTS, PHILOSOPHER

Lights up on an office. Stacey runs into the room, somewhat breathless.

Stacey: You guys, we have no time left! There's none left in the storage room.

Tim: What do you mean, there's none left?

Stacey: I was just in there. It's gone!

Bob: Oh no! Do you think we should borrow some from Accounting?

Tim (answering quickly): No. We'll just be working on borrowed time, and I don't want to do that again.

Stacey: Yeah, you're right. Then it's just a matter of time before we're right back where we started.

Bob: They really didn't have any quality time anyway.

Tim: It was really just a waste of time when I borrowed it.

Bob: Yeah, big time!

Stacey: Well, we really need to start saving time.

A pause before Tim speaks.

Tim: Hey, what time is it, anyway?

Bob: Time for lunch!

All three nod and exit stage right.

Silly, right? The sketch points to a reality many of us unconsciously create and live. We treat time like a finite thing, like books or coffee, that we can run out of or potentially have too much of. In reality, time and the clock are man-made constructs, and we have all the time we need to do the things we really want to do.

In this chapter, we'll explore transformational truths about the nature of time and how we get ourselves into trouble by relating to time from a place of fear: either having too much or not enough. We'll also discuss transactional tips for effectively "managing time" in your personal and professional life.

A TRANSFORMATIONAL LOOK AT TIME

Time is not a commodity. It can't be bought and sold. We won't run out of it in the way we run out of coffee or paper clips (at least not until we finally run out in death). Still, time needs to be worked with in our mind and in our daily lives. Successful time management starts with changing our view of time and, as you've guessed by now, how we relate to it.

WHAT IS TIME?

Time, as we traditionally know it, is a convention. So is the clock, with its system of hours and minutes. We humans created time and the clock to keep ourselves organized and to make society function more smoothly. The mind has a way of ordering events, and overall, this process is helpful. This ordering of events is what gives us the perception of time.

Sir Isaac Newton defined time as a way of measuring

fixed, finite cycles. He believed in an absolute concept of time, that our perception of time cannot be influenced by the way we relate to it. Albert Einstein, on the other hand, saw time as not fixed or finite. In fact, through his theory of relativity, Einstein proved that our experience of time is relative, that it speeds up or slows down depending on our situation. Einstein understood that time doesn't pass at the same rate for each person. We all have an experience of something we label as time, but how quickly or slowly, how enjoyably or painfully, that time passes depends on how we relate to it.[1]

Humans have imaginings that we label as memories so we can think about the past. We also have imaginings that create images of something yet to come, which we label as the future. And we can think about things going on right now, in the present. All of these periods make up an experience that we also label "time."

We first experience stress in our relationship with time when we view it as inherently real. We add to this stress by seeing time as a finite thing. Then we start to relate to time as something that needs to be managed and controlled in and of itself. We think we never have enough time to get everything done. When we relate from fear, we can also think we have too much time and become bored and restless. When we view time from a place of trust, however, we understand that we have all the time we need to do what we want to do and, more importantly, all of the energy to do what we want to do.

RELATING TO TIME

As mentioned in chapter 1, we have a relationship with everything we contact. We also have an initial unbidden reaction. Depending on our state of awareness, we continue the relationship in fear or trust. Our relationship with time is no different. Relating out of fear shows up as a feeling of constriction in our bodies. We will experience this as unpleasant, and we will fall into reactivity. We try to avoid that unpleasant experience.

When we relate from fear, it can feel like time is happening *to* us. In reality, time is only our experience of attempting to order our perception of a past, a future, and the present into some way that makes sense to us and allows us to feel sane. Our experience of an hour or span of minutes, however, depends on our internal frame of mind. Let's say two people arrive at the airport gate ten minutes before boarding. One person might be thinking, "Oh my gosh! I wish I could just get on the plane," while the other person might be thinking, "Man, this is great! I have ten minutes to sit still." Same ten minutes, very different experience.

COMMON MYTHS ABOUT TIME

If we aren't paying attention to how we relate to time, we can start believing several common myths—common because we are all conditioned to believe them, both individually and as organizations. Whenever you realize you're trapped in believing one of these myths, stop, talk to yourself, and remind yourself of the true nature of time.

Not Enough Time

First, we start believing that we don't have enough time. We recycle this thought over and over, which creates more stress. We become like a hamster, running its wheel on adrenaline, stuck in a reactive loop. Life feels like it is speeding up on us, like we can't catch our breath. Believing we don't have enough time springs from the illusion that time is finite. It is one of the most compulsive thought patterns related to time.

If we're stuck in thoughts of not having enough time and believe them, we'll continue creating this experience. Remember Steve from chapter 4? In his mind, Steve replayed the story that his manager didn't appreciate him. Then he acted in a way that made his manager think he didn't need input, which seemed to validate Steve's thoughts. In the same way, if we're stuck in thinking we don't have enough time, we're going to create that experience. It becomes a self-fulfilling prophecy. For example, to maintain the illusion that we don't have enough time to be on time, we might show up late for meetings, or we might find ourselves constantly breaking agreements with other people and not accomplishing tasks we said we would. Psychologist Gay Hendricks said, "You will never have enough time to do the things you don't want to do."[2] When we fill our days with obligations instead of focusing on the things that are important to us and give us enjoyment, time will feel even more scarce.

When I believe I don't have enough time, I'm not present. My wisest actions and choices can only come from the here and now. When stuck in reactivity, I'm not aware of what needs to happen at the moment. I'm not listening or paying attention. I keep going even though I know I need rest. I'm focused on getting this thing over with so I can move on to the next thing. I'm looking for the feeling of having more time when, in fact, there is no way that I can have more time. When I get to that next thing, I find the cycle simply repeats. I again find myself with not enough time and wanting more.

Too Busy

Another myth we believe is that we're too busy. The truth is we often use the idea of busyness to keep ourselves from really paying attention and being present with ourselves. We don't like being present with ourselves for too long. It can be uncomfortable. This is one of the main reasons people don't meditate. The restlessness that arises when most of us step off the hamster wheel is almost too much to bear.

If we haven't learned how to pay attention and bring our attention back when it wanders, our minds will jump all over the place. We then do this thing called busyness, which is often merely the outer reflection of our inner experience. It keeps us from seeing ourselves or what is really happening. When we're constantly moving, we don't pay attention to what's really important to us. We don't take time to consider, "What would give me the most joy right now?" and "What would be the wisest choice?" Decisions made in busyness often result in stress and unhappiness. But we don't have time to figure out why we're stressed. We're too busy!

TRANSFORMING TIME

If you work on training your attention, you will start to notice when you fall into reactivity around time. You might become aware that you feel fearful, stressed, or anxious about how much time you think you do or don't have. As soon as you realize you are in Reactivity Land (relating from fear), try some of the tricks you learned in Part I. Talk to yourself. Ask yourself what's really happening. Remind yourself that the stress you may feel around time is coming from your thoughts—and thoughts aren't reality. The truth is you have all the time you need to do what you want to do. You can choose how you relate to the idea of time and transform your experience. As we've discussed, reactivity is normal. It's what happens after the initial reaction that can get us stuck.

Once you come back to trust and openness, you have options. It's possible that you do need to work on practical transactional skills to keep yourself better organized and keep your next steps clear. After you change your internal mindset, the actions you may need to take in the external world will be more fruitful and effective. They will be more aligned when you're acting from a place of trust versus a place of fear or scarcity. (See the Transacting from Trust section for tips.)

A TRANSACTIONAL LOOK AT TIME

As stated, time is a man-made convention. However, we still live in a time-bound world of meetings and due dates and clocks. To be effective leaders, we need to bring our new mindset into our workplace transactions.

TRANSACTING FROM FEAR

Perhaps you don't think you struggle in your relationship with time. Do you know what fear-driven transaction around time looks like? When leaders transact from fear, they don't take time to create a system or follow an accurate list. They try to multitask, and as we will soon see, they ignore their relationships and the needs of others. As long as we operate from a fear of not having enough time (or having too much time), we won't effectively manage time on the transactional plane, and our teams and leadership interactions will suffer as a result.

No System

Most leaders don't have a practical system for getting things done. They don't know how to make the best use of time because they don't know where their time is going, and when they have time, they don't know how to use it. Because they don't have a reliable list of the day's tasks, they spend a great deal of time thinking and rethinking their next action instead of just acting. When someone asks for a report, they say they'll get on it—but they don't write down this agreement. When someone verbally schedules a meeting, they say they'll be there—but they don't write it down. Most leaders think they can keep it all in their heads, but they can't. It takes too much psychic energy to remember all the things we've agreed to do. We forget what we've said, or we remember at three in the morning when the beautiful mind reminds us of the thing we didn't do.

Faulty List Making

In his book *Getting Things Done*, David Allen says your mind is for having ideas, not holding them.[3] This is a great argument for making lists. We need to get all the stuff we have to do out of our head and onto paper (or the screen).

Most leaders I work with are good at making a list. However, in their list making, most leaders don't distinguish between multistep projects and discrete tasks, so their list is not helpful. Leaders look at their list and mentally check off five things that cannot be done that day because each involves fifty steps, five hours, and the help of thirty other people. They skip those items on their list. Then they get to the end of the day and feel like they haven't accomplished anything because so many items couldn't be checked off. They also feel ineffective because their list contains items that have been there for six months. Instead of an action list, it becomes a disappointment and stress list.

For tips on effective list making, see the later section on Projects versus Tasks and the exercise at the end of the chapter.

Ineffective Multitasking

Another action that comes out of our fear-based relationship to time is multitasking to "save time." We're so afraid of not having enough time that we try to do two or three tasks at once. However, we don't really multitask. We're task switching, moving our attention between two, three, or four things. We check email while participating in a conference call. We check our cell messages while we're at dinner. We text while driving. These actions range from strange to rude to downright dangerous.

Today, our multitasking tendencies are influenced by the multitude of readily available free platforms and technologies. If people had to start paying for Facebook, Instagram, and more, usage would likely drop and these technologies would no longer be such a distraction. As it is, however, these platforms are readily available, seemingly endless, and constantly pulling at our attention.

When our attention shifts to distractions like social media, email, and phone alerts, it can take approximately twenty-five minutes to return our focus to what we were originally working on.[4] Twenty-five minutes! Consider what is happening every time one of those email alerts pops up on your screen or your phone dings at you right in the middle of a conversation. You may think you're multitasking, but you're actually allowing your attention (and your energy) to be managed by others.

Additionally, when we shift our attention back to our original task, we experience "attention residue." Researcher Sophie Leroy coined this term to describe the reality that after we shift our attention back, our minds are still hanging on to distraction we just left.[5] A common result of allowing our attention to be pulled hither and yon is that we ultimately leave things unfinished. Given that we have an innate desire to complete things, the mind will remind us of what we haven't done (known as the Zeigarnik effect[6]), often at three in the morning. This shifting back and forth saps our energy, impedes restful sleep, and often leads to increased anxiety. To manage the energy drain and constant state of having unfinished tasks, we try to work "faster." Now we've got a perfect setup for relating to time from fear.

According to the Killingsworth study mentioned earlier, our experience and happiness are shaped by how present we are. This might also explain the less-than-fulfilling experience we have with our day-to-day lives and tasks when we attempt to multitask.

As the data shows, no one can accurately and effectively complete tasks when they are distracted by buzzes and whistles. We can't do multiple things at once. We're bound to miss something. It might be a question directed at us on a call or a red light. Worse, we create a lot of suffering for ourselves and others with our ineffectiveness that costs us not only our well-being but also potentially money.

Transacting in fear of time and living in the space of distraction thus narrows our mental capacity, or psychic bandwidth. We tunnel our attention and neglect anything outside the tunnel, including interpersonal relationships and other goals. Decision-making skills suffer in this narrowed state.

One study in Princeton Seminary's theology department shows the effects of shrinking bandwidth due to believing that there isn't enough time or the real experience of living at the determinant of the clock. In this Good Samaritan Study, researchers recruited students and divided them into three groups. All three groups had the same task: walk over to another building on campus, meet their team, and practice a sermon they were supposed to deliver.

Group A was told they had plenty of time to walk over to the other building. They were actually running ahead of schedule and would probably arrive early. Group B was told they were on time, but they should head over right away so they wouldn't be late. And Group C was told they were running behind and needed to hustle to arrive on time.

The route between buildings took students through an alleyway that was only four feet across. Partway down the alley, a stranger (an actor) was slumped over on the ground, groaning and writhing in pain. Because the alley was so narrow, students could not pass the stranger without seeing him.

Participants were sent down the alleyway one at a time. Researchers wanted to see how many students would stop to help the stranger and whether the condition of time—early, on time, or nearly late—affected their decision.

Researchers found that 63 percent of the people who thought they were early (Group A) stopped to help the stranger. Of those who thought they were on time (Group B), 45 percent stopped to help. Only 10 percent of the late people in Group C stopped to help.[7]

What do these results show? Time and our experience of it matters. Actually, the students' perception of how much time they had mattered. Researchers concluded that students' experience of having limited time influenced the way they behaved toward another human being. Fear-induced tunnel vision caused them to ignore someone in obvious pain.

The results of time pressure on behavior and decision-making have been replicated in other studies and environments.[8] When people feel like they are living in a scarcity of time, their entire world shifts. Their focus, values, and behaviors narrow. Prosocial behavior is affected, and people who might otherwise be kind and compassionate don't help another human being.

Taxed bandwidth affects interpersonal relationships at work too. If I think I don't have enough time, my number one goal is to avoid that unpleasant feeling. I will prioritize things that *appear* to help me do that. Thus, I will probably prioritize my to-do list over bonding with my team. I'll be less patient, less attentive, and less likely to listen. All of those things take time, which I don't think I have.

Our shrinking mental capacity shows up in our body too. We're perpetually exhausted because we're running on adrenaline.[9] Our stress hormones are out of whack. We don't feel alive. Rather than serving as a warning that something is off, this depleted state often reinforces our thought that we don't have enough time. Our "body budget" and ability to manage our energy matters to us a great deal more than we recognize.[10]

We also try to borrow time from the future. We start putting things off, like playing with our kids, thinking we will do them later. This is faulty thinking. How will we make time later? Why would there be more time later? Thinking we can borrow time shows we are seeing time as finite and limited. It also shows we overvalue the immediate.

We go after the short-term solution rather than what is most beneficial in the long run. Author and educator Stephen Covey talks about this idea and how we spend time on things that seem urgent (e.g., answering the phone when we're in the middle of a conversation, responding to a text while we are driving with our kids in the car), but are mostly unimportant. Instead, he suggests that we focus on what is most important—building relationships, exercising, and getting plenty of sleep.[11] Basically, all the things we know we should do but don't. Yet again, when we are constricted around the idea of time, everything seems important and urgent.

TRANSACTING FROM TRUST

How can you stop these unhealthy behaviors around time? Here are a few suggestions.

Responsibility

The first step is to take responsibility for your relationship with time. This is a choice. Moment by moment, you need to pay attention to how you're relating to time. In your daily interactions with your team, as you look at your schedule for the week (assuming that you do so), as you consider the due dates for upcoming projects—in all these situations and many more, pay attention to your thoughts and emotions around time.

Do you find yourself anxious or thinking "I don't have enough time"? Have you noticed your patience is lagging because you feel pressured by a looming deadline? Have you realized you've completely been ignoring your spouse and kids because of scarcity-induced tunnel vision? Stop. Ask yourself, "What's happening right now? How am I relating to time?" Come back to the present. Remind yourself that time is not a commodity you can run out of. You have all the time you need to do all the things you want.

Remember, practicing mindfulness is a choice. Take responsibility for how you're currently relating to time, and choose to go in a different direction.

Energy Management

As discussed, our relationship with time is what creates our experience of it. Time isn't inherently real. We can't control the hands on the clock or influence the passage of minutes and hours. As a result, we can't really manage time. Instead, we can manage how effective we are in the process of using our energy and attention and getting our work done.

We often forget that our bodies are energy machines that need certain things to function optimally. Managing our energy involves maintaining our bodies in four areas: physical, mental, emotional, and spiritual.

James Loehr and Tony Schwartz studied professional athletes to learn what allowed them to perform at peak or optimal levels. They then translated their discoveries to their work with "corporate athletes."[12] Since everything we do in a day requires energy, our skillfulness in energy usage—pacing ourselves, expending high energy on the appropriate tasks, and so on—makes the difference between performing at an optimal level and limping along.

Another key is having energy reserves to tap into as needed. On a day-to-day basis, most leaders are running on empty. They don't have energy reserves to access for that extra push of concentration or extra ounce of peace in a stressful situation. Loehr and Schwartz found that those athletes (and leaders) who could oscillate between energy expenditure and recovery garnered the greatest success in their lives.

The following five important (though not revolutionary) practices can boost your energy reserves, enable you to effectively manage your energy, and help you get the most out of your time. Please do not let the simplicity of these approaches decrease your belief around their efficacy. Try them for yourself, and see what happens.

1. Maintain a consistent sleep and wake schedule, and go to bed early. For most people, the ideal number of

hours to sleep per night is seven to eight. If you need to get up at 5:00 a.m., for example, an ideal bedtime would be nine to nine-thirty. Consistently staying up until eleven or midnight will result in sleep deprivation. The research on the impact of sleep confirms that being sleep deprived is like driving while inebriated, contributes to negative moods like irritability and fatigue, and can actually make us gain weight.[13]

2. Spend thirty minutes a day being physically active and getting your heart rate elevated. Regular physical activity gives us a plethora of benefits beyond just increasing our physical well-being. It improves our mood and our ability to sleep well. It enhances our stress buffers and allows us to manage stress more effectively. It supports our mental and emotional health as well as our physical.

3. Eat healthy food. At minimum, eating healthy means keeping the processed foods and sugar minimized in the diet. Sugar and carbohydrates are one of the major causes of our current epidemic of obesity and chronic diseases. Removing the excess carbohydrates from the diet can have dramatic effects in reversing Type 2 diabetes and keeping our weight at the optimal level for our body type. Staying at the optimal weight enables our bodies to use less energy in everyday activities.

4. Do those things that make you feel truly good. Spend your time wisely, and use it in ways that will renew

your energy. This may mean taking a walk in the woods or listening to some great music. Find your energy renewers, and engage with them as one of your rituals. For me it's meditating and writing in my journal. Game changer!

5. Manage technology, and don't let technology manage you. As mentioned earlier, multitasking is an energy sapper. We use energy both to shift our attention between tasks and to avoid getting sucked into distractions in the first place. Technology, with its ever-present barrage of buzzes, chimes, and red dots, is the biggest distraction culprit, and we need to proactively manage it so it doesn't steal our energy. Giancarlo Pitocco, former Facebook, Instagram, and Apple digital ad employee, founded his organization Purposeful to address the distraction challenges created by these organizations in their quest to keep us on their platforms as long as possible to show us as many ads as possible. Pitocco advocates that we do the following:

   ◦ Notice how much time you're spending on your device. Did you intend to scroll through Twitter for the past five minutes, or were you scrolling mindlessly?

   ◦ Experiment with removing notifications and see what happens. You can always turn them back on.

   ◦ Test the story you may have about needing to reply to requests immediately. See what happens to your boundaries and how they might naturally change for the better.[14]

We can manage our energy with regular practices of rest and renewal and building reserves so we can keep the tank full and ready to go. This type of energy management makes our experience of time change in dramatic ways.

Job Crafting

Even in the realm of choosing what we want to do and saying no to the things that we don't, our roles at work can often seem to take on a life of their own. We may find ourselves doing too much of what we don't necessarily enjoy, which can impact our experience of time. Remember, we'll never have enough time to do the things we don't want to do.

An interesting approach to this dilemma is the skill of job crafting, or redesigning work to cultivate more satisfaction and enjoyment. Job crafting enables us to create a more pleasing use of our time while working. Psychologists Amy Wrzesniewski and Jane Dutton discovered that people naturally change their job descriptions to fit their values and preferences.[15] This, in turn, allows people to find a deeper meaning in their work. Take the barista at my local coffee shop, for example. While making orders quickly and accurately is part of his actual job, he adds a key element. As he says, "I help people get off to the best start of their day." He has changed his job description to include sending people off on the right foot because that gives himself pleasure and meaning.

According to Wrzesniewski and Dutton, there are three ways to consider crafting your work:

1. If possible, take on fewer tasks (especially those that you don't enjoy), or take on more tasks that you do enjoy. You may also decrease or increase the scope of certain tasks by delegating. For example, when working on a project, you might need to collect a ton of data and input it into a spreadsheet. Instead of doing the entire data entry yourself, you could delegate parts of it to your team. Or maybe tracking and reporting needs to be completed. Instead of defaulting to weekly reporting, you switch to a once-every-two-weeks schedule. You can also change the way you complete certain tasks, like listening to enjoyable music when completing a more mundane part of your work.
2. Create more connection with people you enjoy working with. Look for the opportunity to collaborate with those who bring you positive energy.
3. Take a bigger view of the tasks you perform. Changing your perception about your work and how it impacts

everyone around you shifts the meaning behind the actions you take. Similar to my favorite neighborhood barista, you can consider how your work as a leader impacts the people you lead. Remind yourself of the hopes, dreams, and aspirations of your team members, and see how you can contribute.[16]

Spend a few moments thinking about how you can sculpt the way in which you work. Doing so can make it feel as though time is flying by, bring you greater energy, and allow you to gain more effectiveness and efficiency.

Projects versus Tasks

Taking responsibility for our relationship with time is key in shifting our mindset. However, even if we internally relate to time from a place of trust, we still need to know how to externally organize the stuff to be done.

David Allen, author of *Getting Things Done*, suggests people learn to distinguish between tasks and projects. A task is one discrete step or action. A project is anything that requires more than one step.[17]

On your to-do list, for example, you might write "Send a birthday card to my brother." In theory, that sounds like a simple task, but let's break it down.

First, you need to get a card. (You could shortcut this step by using an e-card, but it's still going to be more than one step.) Next, you have to make sure you have your brother's address. If you don't, you have to get it, which could involve calling Mom or texting a sibling. You have to find a stamp. You need to write a message to your brother, or at the very least sign your name. You need to put the card in the mail.

When you take all those steps into consideration, sending a birthday card to your brother is not a task; it's a multi-step project. Each of the discrete steps—buying the card, signing it, mailing it—is a task. Some steps have dependencies (you have to buy the card before you can sign it), while others don't (you can buy the stamps and find the address before you buy the card and sign it).

As David Allen says, we do tasks, not projects. When we write our to-do list, we actually need to write two separate lists—one for projects and one for tasks—and then work from the task list. The exercise at the end of this chapter will help you create a project list and a task list.

Once you've got your task list sorted out, start a daily practice of identifying the top three things you want to get done. Be realistic in terms of the amount of time and resources needed for each item. Not sure which task to tackle first? Some people like to start with the easiest tasks; others like to tackle the hardest things first. In his book *Eat That Frog*, Brian Tracy suggests identifying the thing you really don't want to do and do that first.[18] Try different tactics, and find out what works best for you.

One reason you may feel overwhelmed in looking at your daily to-do list is that it's filled with multistep projects that can't realistically be completed in one day or it contains steps that need to be taken before other steps can be handled. As a result, you don't have many items checked off at the end of the day. Thinking projects are tasks that can leave you feeling like you're not getting things done, and I've never met a leader who enjoys that feeling.

Sometimes we're not aware of all the steps, time, and resources involved in any given project. Sometimes we don't remember all the projects we're involved in at some level. We say yes to things and then don't remember we did so. Or we say yes to things we shouldn't because we are unaware of how full our plate is and we keep going to the buffet of life to put more things on it. Time is a convention, and we can only be in one place at a time, so we can't schedule two meetings on Thursday at 3:00 p.m. We need to keep track of the things that we've agreed to.

Calendars and To-Do Lists

In their daily execution of tasks, many leaders try to stuff thirty pounds of crap into a ten-pound bag. Then they complain about it, but they just keep trying to stuff the same amount of crap (tasks) into the same size bag (eight or ten hours). Instead, they should look for ways to become more efficient and effective.

For example, you could give yourself a bigger bag. Giving yourself a bigger bag might be adopting a different mindset or saying no so that you have less stuff to put in it. This is an excellent start, but you still need to know how to become a more effective time user. Many leaders I work with don't have a realistic view of how many hours it takes to perform a task at a high level. The result is trying to stuff too many actions into too little space.

For example, I was traveling for work and one of my clients wanted to go out to dinner the night of my arrival. He offered to pick me up at the airport and then head straight to dinner. As we were lingering over drinks and chatting, his wife called. He politely said, "Oh, let me take this. It's my wife. I told her I'd be home around six." I looked at my watch. It was 6:20. After he got off the phone I said, "You told her six? My flight didn't land until four forty-five. How did you think we would leave the airport and get to dinner and finish eating in time for you to be home by six? Also, stop breaking agreements with your wife." He looked at me a bit dumbfounded for a minute and said, "I guess I thought we'd have more time." Thus, we need to have a realistic view.

After you have separated tasks from projects, determine the top three tasks that need to be completed that day. Then look at your calendar. If you have four back-to-back meetings, you likely won't be able to do X, Y, and Z from your task list. You have to be realistic.

Also, there's no substitute for blocking out one to two hours a day on your calendar to make sure you can tackle your task list. You have to carve out that time. Put each block in your calendar, and stick to it so no one can schedule something over it.

Finally, constantly update your lists. They are moving targets. The most important item people forget is that this is not a set-it-and-forget-it situation. Get into a routine of picking three items a day, checking your calendar daily, and reviewing your lists. If you want to change your transactional relationship to time, you need to adopt some kind of routine. Without a new plan and a commitment to keep doing it, we will simply revert to our normal patterns.

You also have to consider your system for list keeping— paper or electronic. Paper moves quickly, but it becomes messy because you end up with multiple pages. Electronic is cleaner and the systems tend to make it easier to stay organized, but it can move slower if you're in a place that doesn't have great connections or you have to learn the software. It can also require you to stay connected with your device more than you'd like. Recall the segment on our attention economy.

Planner systems and project management tools abound. Some of my favorite systems (beyond *Getting Things Done* by David Allen) and tools include the Franklin Covey Planner, the Full Focus Planner by Michael Hyatt, Asana, Omni Focus, and Basecamp. In addition, there are many time management techniques, such as the Pomodoro Technique, that help us work with time instead of against it. The system itself doesn't matter except to you as the end user. What matters is that you have a trusted system that works and that you use it daily. I suggest people use a system that brings them joy. Ask yourself, "Do I like looking at it? Do I like working in it?"

When you make this shift, it will be messy at first. You'll feel like you're not getting it. If you're tempted to quit, remember the transformational truths. Remember why your relationship with time matters. You no longer want to live in fear of time.

Ben Franklin once said, "Time is money." In the next chapter, we'll consider the connection between these two phenomena and ways to transform your thoughts and actions around the almighty dollar.

EXERCISE: PROJECT VERSUS TASK

Goal: This exercise will help you distinguish between a project and a task. As a result, you will be able to create more realistic to-do lists.

Process: Write down everything that's swimming around in your head. Everything you have to do at work, at home, in your volunteer work, for your hobby—everything. This is the mind dump. Don't make distinctions in the kinds of tasks or numbers of steps. Just write it all down in one long list.

After your mind dump, go through and put an asterisk (*) next to all the things that require more than one step (i.e., projects). Remember the birthday card example: anything that requires more than one discrete step is a project, not a task.

Now divide your mind dump list into two separate lists, one for projects and one for tasks.

After you have two separate lists, you can break down projects into tasks and then move the individual tasks onto the task list. Use the task list to determine your daily to-do list.

At the beginning of each day, look at your task list and identify the top three things you want to get done. Be realistic in terms of the amount of time and resources needed for each item.

Once you've got your top three things, you're ready to go. Work from your list every day. This will keep you from having to rethink what to do next when you finish one of your tasks. Additionally, get in the habit of adding tasks to your list as you think of them, rather than trying to keep them in your head.

At least once per week, update your task list. Delete the tasks you've accomplished, remove tasks that are no longer on your plate, and identify what still needs to be done. Remember, this list is a living, breathing thing, and it will change as much as you do. It isn't static, and that's what keeps it exciting and fun!

CHAPTER 6

MONEY

"It is not the man who has too little, but the man who craves more, that is poor."

—SENECA

"If I had known what it would be like to have it all, I might have been willing to settle for less."

—LILY TOMLIN

I will never forget the day I drove to the corporate office to tell my boss I was resigning. The day I was willing to walk away from about $2 million.

I had a meeting scheduled to discuss the post-acquisition organizational structure.

"We're going to make you a vice president," Tim said as he slid the org structure across the desk. "Here's the new org structure. I know your name isn't on it."

"Well, that's interesting," I replied as I glanced at the page.

"Well, you know, org structures are hard."

I pushed the chart back across the desk and said, "Well, how about this. I'm going to do you one better. I'm going to resign."

"What's that?"

"I'm going to resign my position. I'm happy to stay on in a consulting role to teach leadership development, but I will no longer be a full-time employee."

Tim sat back in his chair and said, "Well, that's different."

"Yeah," I said.

And with that, I walked out into the great unknown.

A lot of internal transformation took place before I quit. I had to unhook myself from my fear-based relationship with money, a process that took several years. Even though I had plenty of money in the bank, I still lived with a fear of not having enough. I also feared that if I quit my job to do something else, I would never make as much as I was at the time. In addition, I was a partner in the company, with a beautiful pair of "golden handcuffs." If I walked away, I would lose the gold. Or so I believed.

Then I looked at the facts in my relationship with money: I put myself through college, I have a doctorate, I will always be able to get a job, I have never struggled for money as an adult, and I seemed to be able to earn a good living for myself. Once I looked at what was true, I was able to pull myself out of the story that I wouldn't have enough. That's what finally gave me the courage to quit, along with the transactional move of meeting with a financial advisor to determine how much money I really needed to save to be able to retire at age fifty.

About a year after meeting with the financial advisor, I quit.

This chapter will help you think through how you relate to money. It will also give you tips on transacting more wisely in the business world. We'll start by looking at the link in our relationships with time and money.

TIME–MONEY CONNECTION

When Ben Franklin said, "Time is money," he was speaking to a tradesman. In essence, he was saying, "If you're not out earning ten pence, you might as well take ten pence and throw it in the ocean." This philosophy doesn't play out in our modern world because most organizations have paid time off. In other words, workers can go play and get paid for it. Additionally, time versus money is a false dichotomy. It's like we're comparing apples and oranges.

Modern workers have more discretionary time than they've ever had. Researchers Mark Aguiar and Erik Hurst evaluated over five decades of time-use studies based on commonly used household surveys that document trends in the allocation of time. Their findings suggest that between 1965 and 2005, men's leisure time increased by six to nine hours per week and women's leisure time rose by four to eight hours per week.[1]

Yet leaders and workers still feel as though they don't have enough time. In 2016, researcher Ashley Whillans and her team analyzed a survey that asked 2.5 million Americans about their leisure time. They found that 80 percent of respondents felt they don't have enough time to do the things they want to do. In other words, they are time poor.[2]

Research shows that if we really want to increase our capacity for joy, calm, and less stress, we need to start using money as a means to experience our time in the way we would like. We also need to value our time more than our money.[3]

For example, spending our time and energy doing things we don't want to do negatively impacts our experience of time, making it seem long and drawn out. To counteract this experience, we can use our monetary resources to "buy back" time. How do we buy time? Hire someone to do the things we don't want to do. Find someone to clean the house. Pay a neighbor kid to wash the car. Hire a grocery delivery service or a meal prep service. By paying someone to do these things, we place a greater value on our time than the money itself. When we relate to money from fear, we lose sight of this reality. In that state, the idea of paying someone to do something we don't want to do seems frivolous and extravagant.

We sometimes have a hard time paying for services we could, in theory, do ourselves. However, in situations where we don't feel qualified to complete the task at hand—to fix an electrical problem, for example—we have no problem paying another person to do the task. Could I learn how to install my own electrical outlets? Absolutely. Would that take a lot of my valuable time to learn to do so? Absolutely. Is that how I want to experience my time? Definitely not. So, I hire an expert to do the work. In this instance, paying someone to do that work makes a lot of sense.

In addition to paying an expert for his or her expertise, however, we're also paying to experience time how we want to experience it. I don't want to spend my time learning to install an electrical outlet. I would rather go to the beach. In this sense, hiring an expert is no different from paying someone to mow the lawn, wash the car, or any other task we are "qualified" to do but don't want to. Either way, we're buying time so we can spend it the way we want.

Additionally, consider this: I can actually earn more money doing what I love and what I've been educated to do, and then use that cash to hire the electrician or the cleaning person or the grocery service. The time I would "spend" doing things I don't enjoy, and that I'm not trained to do, isn't worth the energy.

Valuing our time in relationship to money is tricky. It's easier to measure the value of $10,000 than an extra thirty or sixty minutes. However, when we realize that how we use our time impacts our well-being, we can more easily see the value of paying for a service that will free time for stargazing or mountain climbing or whatever gives us joy and positive emotion.

At the root of our relationship with money is one erroneous belief: that having more money will make us happier. Studies have found that even individuals with a net worth of $10 million think they need to dramatically increase their wealth to be happy.[4] Money does contribute to our overall satisfaction with life, but only up to a certain point. Research by Daniel Kahneman and Angus Deaton allows us to understand more about the ways in which we become dismayed by the time-money paradox.[5]

Most people consider their level of well-being in one of two ways: based on emotions (e.g., Do I feel good right now? Did I enjoy that interaction?) or evaluations (e.g., life is good right now or things are not going well). Kahneman and Deaton asked people if having more money made them happier along these two aspects of well-being. People reported increasing emotional and evaluative well-being up to earnings of approximately $75,000 a year. Beyond this number, people may evaluate their life as more satisfying, but interestingly, their emotional life is the same as those who earn $75,000. Therefore, more money doesn't in fact, make us feel happier or give us access to more positive emotion.

As I've experienced repeatedly in my own life and seen in the lives of many high-income earners I've had the pleasure to work with, increased consumption often results in diminishing returns. Many leaders come to me befuddled by the stark reality that they have worked many years to earn a lot of money only to find themselves no happier and, oftentimes, less happy than they have ever been. The story goes, "I thought that once I earned all of this money, I'd finally be able to relax. I'd be happier." They realize that they were rolling the dice on a losing bet.

At the same time, people believe they need more money to be happy, but they can't give a figure of exactly how much. When I ask leaders how much money they actually need to live comfortably in retirement, most cannot give me an actual figure. We've bought into this idea that we don't have enough, but we don't even know what enough is.

A TRANSFORMATIONAL LOOK AT MONEY

When I met with the financial planner before I quit, we discussed legacy wealth and giving to charitable causes. It suddenly hit me: how much money have I ever given away? What could I be giving away now? Because I had been living in a fear-based reality of not having enough money, being generous with my funds had never dawned on me. I had never thought of contributing monetarily to something bigger than myself. This also is a reality found in the research. When we prioritize and focus on money, our behavior changes. We become less helpful, a bit stingier, and less interested in the welfare of our fellow man.[6] Money motivates us to work more hours, but it decreases our motivation to help others.

After realizing how I had been functioning, I decided

to do an experiment. I stopped looking at my checking account for a year. In doing so, I unchained myself from the dot. I stopped compulsively looking at the balance and stressing about running out. Because I wasn't worried about the balance, I actually gave away more during that year and still ended up having more than enough. I proved to myself that obsessing over money doesn't help.

After that year, I stopped relating to money out of fear. I stopped trying to hold on to it. I realized money is meant to flow and that it comes and goes. Like all things in life, money isn't permanent. Attempting to hold on to it is as ridiculous as trying to hold on to good feelings. But out of fear, we still try, with all our might. The truth is, if it flows out, it's going to flow back in, so there's no need to worry.

When we relate to money from fear, we start believing things that aren't true. Then we act on those beliefs.

WHAT IS MONEY?

Like time, money is a convention or construction. We started using money because it was easier than walking around with a stack of beaver pelts. In the past, people would trade pelts for other goods, like oranges. However, if the orange seller ran out, the buyer with pelts had to go elsewhere for fruit. The bartering system had limits. When the bartering system became less useful, humans created a system using coins and then paper currency with assigned values. Everyone could get what they needed as long as they had enough pieces of metal or paper.

COMMON MYTHS ABOUT MONEY

The problem is that we can start relating to the paper money from a place of fear. We're driven to work more and more to accumulate as many pieces of paper as we can. At some level, we believe money will run out someday, and we will never be able to have more. We start hoarding paper currency to make sure we always have enough to get what we need and, often, more than we need.

In our fear-based state, we also believe more is better. We convince ourselves that if we accumulate lots of pieces of paper, we will experience never-ending happiness and joy. A tyranny of advertising feeds this fear. We don't need one pair of pants; we need fifty. We need the latest and greatest car with all the gadgets. We live in a world of things, and we are convinced we must have them all. Having a lot of things requires money, lots of it. Herein lies the toxicity in our relationship with money and the searing heat of greed.

In our world today, we also experience the paradox of

choice.[7] The multitude of choices drives consumerism, and the need for more money. It simultaneously decreases our well-being. We're driven by the need to have the *best* car or go to the *best* college, but how do we decide which is best? It's impossible. We spend a lot of energy trying to accomplish the impossible, and we sacrifice our well-being in the process.

All of these myths are based on fear, and the root idea is we don't have enough, there's not going to be enough, and it's all going to disappear, along with our happiness. Because we relate to money from this place of fear, we start experiencing money in this way. Our thoughts create our experience.

GRATITUDE

Gratefulness is one of the keys to unhooking yourself from a fear-based relationship to money. Be grateful for the resources you have right now, because right now is all there is. Focus on what you have available in the present, not what you're missing or what you think you won't have in the future. When we're not grateful, it seems like nothing will meet our need. Everything is a black hole, so we keep striving for more.

As we've learned, the mind's propensity and naturally wired negativity bias not only makes the difficult times hit us harder but it also slants our predictions toward what could go wrong. The practice of gratitude tunes our attention to what is going right in life and, more so, what we are thankful for. Gratitude is a celebration of the now.

I put myself through college, and when I say there were days, weeks, and months that I had no idea how I was going to pay the rent or pay for classes, I am not exaggerating. It was stressful, to say the least. However, even in those moments, I was grateful for the money I did have. I could at least buy steak sauce and flour tortillas to eat for dinner (which I did on more than one occasion). I also recall feeling grateful for my health and for having a body that would let me go out into the world and find more work to generate more money. Gratitude helps us generate positive emotion, which broadens our perspective, which in turn gives us access to more internal resources and choices as well as resilience.

Beyond supporting us individually to overcome our individual focus on our lack of money, practicing gratitude also has some major benefits at work. In a survey of two thousand Americans conducted by the John Templeton Foundation, 93 percent of respondents said that grateful bosses were more likely to be successful. Shockingly, however, 60 percent of respondents reported they rarely expressed gratitude at work. While the reasons for this lack of gratitude are likely many, the reality is that practicing gratitude has been shown to contribute greatly to our well-being.[8] In my own life and in my work with clients—especially in managing the relationship to money—I have experienced gratitude as a fundamental practice for working with and overcoming our propensity to focus on what isn't going well.

Here are some specific ways that you can cultivate gratitude in your life, and not only as it pertains to money:

- Say thank you more often, especially if you're the boss. Hearing thank you amps the positive emotion, and hearing it from the boss really impacts people's ability to feel confident and builds trust.[9] Saying thank you with sincerity doesn't cost any money, yet it provides great benefits.
- Record three good things. At the end of each day, take a moment to write down three good things that happened in that day and why they happened. Studies have shown that doing this every day for one week will increase positive emotion.
- Write a gratitude letter. Give consideration to the people in your life who have been a benefactor to you, and write them a letter of appreciation. This is especially impactful if you read the letter to the person.[10]
- Keep a gratitude journal. Writing down the things you are grateful for and sharing these with someone who

is important to you can be a wonderful way to regularly bring gratitude into your life. The difference between a gratitude journal and the three good things exercise is that in your journal, you are not limited to writing about three things. You can write freely about one thing you're grateful for, or many.

· Pay the grateful debit. As you pay bills or pay a vendor, give a special acknowledgment of thanks for the resource you were able to utilize. As I pay my monthly household bills or buy groceries, I often give a momentary pause to consider how fortunate I am to be able to pay for electricity and to even have electricity in my life to allow my house to be illuminated at night and to keep warm and dry.

All of these intentional practices tune our attention to that which is here right now and to the resources that we have available to us each and every moment. There is no waiting for the future (or our joy) to arrive.

A TRANSACTIONAL LOOK AT MONEY

Believing fear-based myths about money can drive us to adverse actions. It can lead us to cut corners in the name of saving a few bucks, especially when saving that money directly affects us.[11] It can also lead to greed on a grand scale. Many companies have gone bankrupt as a result of fraud and illegal financial transactions. When we learn to relate from trust, however, we can let money flow and use it to be a blessing to others.

TRANSACTING FROM FEAR

Fear causes us to make decisions that do not support our well-being or the well-being of those around us. Because of my fear of not having enough money, I stayed in my position for years, even though I was miserable. My decision also impacted my family and friends because I rarely saw them, and when I did, I wasn't the most enjoyable person to be around.

Fear also causes leaders to make decisions that negatively impact the organization. If a company loses a lot of money on one deal, management might decide to "save" money by cutting the entire marketing budget. However, this might be the time when marketing is most needed to increase sales. As with time, fear can produce narrowed vision. Decisions made in this scarcity mindset are usually short-sighted and fail to take in the whole organizational picture.

If we remember the negativity bias, we know that losses hit us harder than gains, and this holds true with money too. If we're faced with the prospect of losing ten dollars or gaining ten dollars, we'll often choose the less risky option to make sure we don't lose the money even if the same level of risk exists with potentially gaining money. Economist Daniel Kahneman has researched how people relate to money, and he found much of that relationship is fear-based. People don't care about not gaining; they just don't want to lose anything.[12]

Sometimes organizations offer bonuses for extra projects. Wanting the money, people take on the projects, which then eat up an additional twenty hours of their week. Then they're faced with not having enough time to do the things they want to do. They tell themselves it'll be worth it when they get paid. And then it's not. They're not any happier. Spending the extra time with money at the forefront of the cause didn't create the joy they thought it would. In addition, they just gave away a bunch of time, which creates more stress and impedes their well-being. When we relate to money from fear, we fail to see that the experience of the task itself matters as much as, if not more than, the money.[13]

Worse yet, when people focus on money over the experience and the intrinsic value of the task itself, they are less likely to spend their time on work they won't be compensated for or on prosocial behaviors such as volunteerism.[14]

Nowhere is the reaction from fear clearer than in our relationship with money. When we get a little money, it feels good and we want to hang on to it. We don't want to lose it. We horde it. When we lose money, we don't want that to happen again. We'll do anything to prevent future losses.

When we're stuck in that cycle, we spread the emotional contagion. Our well-being suffers, and so does everyone around us. As leaders, if we're miserable in our relationship with money and our well-being isn't being taken care of, we'll make decisions to "get mine" that will not be from a place of wisdom and clarity. The decisions we make in a contracted, narrowed state driven by greed will affect our team's well-being, as well as our own.

Greed

Greed is the essence of wanting to hang on to something and unconsciously feeling that we need to have more of it to be happy. We typically use the word *greed* in reference to money, but we can crave anything: time, joy, attention.

When leaders experience greed around money, they feel the need to hang on to it or get more of it. As a result, they might fudge the books or lie to the stockholders. Consider Exhibit A, Bernie Madoff. In 2009, Madoff pleaded guilty to eleven federal felonies related to the massive Ponzi scheme he ran through his wealth management firm. In total, he robbed $65 billion from investors. Misrepresenting and lying are born out of a company's or individual's belief system. Even companies that have access to a great deal of money and the ability to generate more can fall into the trap of fear and greed.

Consider the instances where companies—and the people in charge of them—have acted fraudulently, illegally, and unethically out of greed. Their actions have negatively affected thousands of individuals.[15]

- Enron, 2001: Ken Lay, CEO and board chairman of Enron, and Jeff Skilling, Enron CEO, manipulated financial profits and losses to make the company appear more profitable. Accounting firm Arthur Andersen, which oversaw Enron's accounts, also signed off on the less-than-stable accounting practices being used by Enron. Eventually, the SEC took action after suspecting a lack of transparent reporting. It is estimated that shareholders lost up to $74 billion and that employees lost billions in retirement pension benefits. Accounting firm Arthur Andersen dissolved as a result of the Enron scandal. As of 2017, lawsuits continued against the firm and its partners in crime. Lay could have faced up to forty-five years in prison but died of a heart attack before sentencing. Skilling was sentenced to twenty-four years in prison.[16]
- WorldCom, 2002: CEO Bernard Ebbers and CFO Scott Sullivan manipulated the financial records and reported faulty earnings. All the while, Ebbers was

earning approximately $37 million a year. Ebbers and Sullivan wiped out a firm that once had $103.9 billion on its books. Fifty thousand employees filed a class-action lawsuit to attempt to recoup the billions of dollars lost in their pensions and were awarded $51 million in 2004. Ebbers was sentenced to twenty-five years in prison, while Sullivan was sentenced to five years in a plea agreement to testify against Ebbers.[17]

- Fannie Mae, 2006: Fannie Mae was identified as a "good to great" company in Jim Collins's book *Good to Great*. Collins looked at what certain "good" companies did that contributed to them outpacing stock market returns for a sustained period of time, therefore making them seem great. However, if you would have invested in their stock at the time of the book's release in 2001, you would have suffered an 80 percent loss by 2008. There are many market reasons for losses of this magnitude, but in this case, greed, fraud, and the desire for permanence had the greatest impact. In 2006, Fannie Mae paid the FCC $400 million to settle charges of misstating financial statements from 1998 to 2004. Executives' decisions to lie about the high-risk loans they had taken on heavily contributed to the housing market crash of 2008, which impacted taxpayers across the board.[18]

In the study "To Help or Not to Help: The Good Samaritan Effect and the Love of Money on Helping Behavior," researchers expanded on the earlier Good Samaritan study on time and helping behavior cited in chapter 5. They incorporated people's view of money, instead of time, to see what effect it had on their willingness to help others at work.

In the earlier study, the perception of having less time decreased people's willingness to stop and help a stranger. In the "To Help or Not to Help" money study, 833 organizational professionals were surveyed and asked questions as they pertained to motives of helping behavior, self-reported helping behavior, and the Money Ethic Scale. The Money Ethic Scale was used to understand how an individual's relationship to money may or may not impact their helping behaviors. That is, if I prioritize money and getting my work done over my own intrinsic or altruistic motivators, I may not be as eager to provide assistance to one of my coworkers. The results revealed that those who had a stronger love of money were more extrinsically motivated to help others than those who didn't. In other words, those with a stronger love of money would help only if it seemed to better their individual, overall situation, especially as it related to earning more money. For example, if it made them look good in front of the boss and might get them a promotion. In this way, the love of money indirectly undermines helping behavior.[19]

One could argue that if you want to get helping behaviors from people who don't have their own intrinsic motivation, money might be the motivator to do it. The problem is that you can't always do that in an organization. For example, there are only so many promotions. There is only so much attention I can get from my boss.

In an organization, if workers are only helping because they're getting paid (or getting a bonus) and then payment stops, they will stop their helping behaviors. And as cited earlier, when money is given primary attention over the intrinsic value of the task itself, people are less likely to spend their time on work they won't be compensated for, including helping their colleagues. When people stop helping each other, the culture of the organization suffers. In addition, when people stop helping each other, they cut themselves off from connecting on a deeper level and developing friendships. The critical discovery is that just as our relationship to time influences our helping behaviors, so does our relationship to money.

TRANSACTING FROM TRUST

Unhooking yourself from the myths about money doesn't mean you give all your money away and live on nothing. You still need to be skillful in how you transact with money in the external, both personally and professionally. It's not enough to change our mindset; we need to act skillfully.

Get a Realistic View

If you want to know what you value, look at your checkbook or Venmo account. Where are you spending your money? That's what's most important to you. You're consciously or unconsciously choosing those things. This part of the book contains expected suggestions about saving money and managing our financial health, but first and foremost, we need to have a realistic view and ask ourselves if we are putting our financial resources where we really want them to go.

This is true for organizations too. When organizations say they care about their employees, company culture, and leadership development, I ask for their budget's line-item amount for these things. The number one answer is zero. They may say culture and leadership development are important, but if they haven't budgeted any money toward these things, they're not. If your company or organization isn't willing to put resources (time and money) toward development, it's not important to them. This isn't a judgment statement; it's simply a matter of seeing what's true.

A new movement known as FIRE (Financial Independence, Retire Early) speaks to what one group of people values. The movement mainly consists of people in the millennial generation who are choosing to live on an annual income that may be significantly less than what they're actually earning. They focus on minimizing expenses and saving aggressively to attain enough money for living expenses in perpetuity with the intent of retiring early. The core idea of how much savings a person needs to retire in this movement is based on the results of the Trinity Study, which suggest that a person has sufficient savings if 4 percent of her assets can cover a year's worth of expenses.[20] What is the annual income people need to live their greatest well-being? The data suggest that number is $75,000 to $80,000, as previously stated. Given this amount, the suggested 4 percent number seems plausible, although the evidence for the long-term overall success of this movement is yet to be seen. Additionally, the FIRE movement might not work if you live in expensive states like California, but it's definitely feasible for most states in the Union, and the great news is that most of us can choose where to live.

Individuals in the FIRE movement have decided they don't need to buy everything brand new. They don't need the nicest furniture or two cars. They cook at home more than they go out. They save the money they're not spending, and they choose to spend much less. They already know how much they need to live on during retirement because they've already been living on $80,000 a year. They aren't overworked because they're chasing an unknown figure for retirement. In essence, they're valuing their time and leisure space over money.

Save Money

Money may be energy that's meant to flow, but it's still wise to have money in your checking account so you can pay bills and relax a bit more, knowing that there's enough for unexpected expenses as well. It's also a good idea to have money in your savings account. Some experts suggest having at least six months' worth of expenses saved up. If you're not there yet, don't worry. Now you have a goal to work toward. In terms of retirement, figure out how much you need, realistically, and save toward that goal. It's possible to do these things without getting sucked into fear and reactivity.

Know Your Number

I had a client named Jamie who was a Pilates instructor and massage therapist. During one conversation, I asked him what his monthly number was; in other words, what he needed to earn in a month to pay bills and enjoy life. He had no idea. I suggested he figure it out.

Once Jamie had that number in his head, he was a different person. He suddenly started generating clients and saving money. His whole relationship with money was simplified. He knew his number, and he went after it. He understood what money was supporting in his life. The game changer for Jamie was using money to live his values. One thing he valued was traveling. Jamie set his eyes on saving enough money to travel abroad twice within that year and achieved it. Living your values leads to increased happiness when it comes to money.

The way we are spending our money, or earning it, is also how we are spending our time, or using it. Our relationship with money is never actually about the money. We can use money as an excuse for many things, but truly, it's never really about that. It's about how we see ourselves in the world. In most of the examples where people committed fraud, those individuals already had a lot of money, as did their organizations. Their actions were about status and how they were perceived. Their actions were about control and maintaining the idea of who they thought they were in the world in a cohesive, constructed way. The bottom line was greed, fear, and delusion constructed around an identity. The same was true for me in terms of quitting my job. I didn't know who I'd be if I weren't Daphne, director of leadership development. We will talk about our relationship with the self next.

EXERCISE: THE PAY-OFFS

Goal: This exercise involves three ways to cultivate the biggest pay-offs to our well-being when we are using our financial resources and spending our money.

Process: At the beginning of each month, plan for and execute one of these three actions:

1. Share a gift. Who could you spend some money on this month? It could be a family member, a friend, or a person in line behind you at the coffee shop. The impact of prosocial spending in this way has been shown to benefit our well-being.

2. Buy an experience. What experience would you like to invest in this month that would be enjoyable and aligned with your values? It could be going to a concert or traveling abroad. It could also be as simple as going on a day trip with family or friends.

3. Buy some time. What could you pay someone else to do for you this month that could give you some of your time back? Maybe it's grocery shopping or running some errands or even getting your laundry done. Remember: when we get our time back, we support another person in earning some money. And thus, money flows as it should.

CHAPTER 7

THE SELF

"I always wanted to be somebody, but now I realize I should have been more specific."

—LILY TOMLIN

"Everything you see I owe to spaghetti."

—SOPHIA LAUREN

Meet Betty, CEO of Company Z. Betty started her health-care company when she was nearly forty. Ten years later, the company was thriving. Betty, however, was sleep deprived and anxiety ridden. She was also using alcohol to relax and subsequently developed a drinking problem. She was up at 5:00 a.m. every day, drinking coffee by 5:05, and checking email by 5:15. She worked until eight or nine at night, and then had a nightly bedside beer.

After I started working with Betty, she slowly began

waking up to what was happening. She started realizing that she was entirely too attached to who she believed she was in the world. Failure was not an option. She was a person who got things done, and she believed she had to do everything herself. She believed people were depending on her to take care of all the details, so she was carrying the weight of the world on her shoulders. She believed that the way she had become successful her entire life was by taking on extra responsibility and doing everything on her own. That was her identity: the successful person who gets it all done.

The truth was, she had been successful her whole life. Betty received the Alumni Achievement Award from her preparatory high school and was a two-sport scholarship athlete at a major university. She owned multiple rental properties and had won several industry recognition awards. But Betty had gotten caught up in who she thought she needed to be.

Being successful wasn't a problem. The problem for Betty was that doing all those things to be successful was no longer a choice. Her behavior was driven by a need to maintain the belief about who she had to be and who she was in the world.

Certain factors would have added to Betty's quality of life: normal amounts of sleep, having friends, being able to say no, working forty or even fifty hours a week instead of eighty. But in her mind, these weren't options. Even though Betty was exhausted and creating an addiction for herself that included work and chemical dependency, she couldn't be the person who got enough sleep. Her identity was wrapped around an image that required ridiculous hours of work to maintain.

The aha moment for Betty was when her relationship eroded and she divorced. She had success by the world's standard, but she was deeply unhappy and unfulfilled. At that point, she realized she needed to change.

Betty could actually be called Every Leader. Her story is the path of almost every successful leader I've worked with (myself included, as you learned earlier). They're attached to their success, their image, their control, and as a result, they're not free to choose. This is a key point. Fear gives us no choice. It clouds our vision and lulls us to sleep with its never-ending song of certain doom and the desire to control all that is uncontrollable. It keeps us chained to the dot.

This chapter is about learning to unhook yourself from who you think you are and need to be. The key is seeing your identity as it truly is: unfixed, always changing, and therefore, impermanent like everything else. When you see this transformational truth, you will be free to lead with compassion for yourself and others.

A TRANSFORMATIONAL LOOK AT THE SELF

Betty's story has a happy ending. She let go of the idea that she needed to do everything herself. She started developing other members of her team and delegating many areas she was controlling. She stopped working eighty hours a week.

Betty's change didn't happen all at once. She started by making small choices. First, she started paying attention to what was really going on; namely, that she was working herself ragged trying to maintain the identity of Successful Betty, who does everything and always wins. She realized she was telling herself a story about who she needed to be. She also believed incorrectly that she alone was creating the success. In fact, Betty had an entire team around her making the results possible. Once she started waking up to reality, she realized the products got to market without her being part of every step. Various causes and conditions came together, 99 percent of which she had no control over. This is an often-missed truth when it comes to our identity: we believe we are the doer and miss the deeper truth about all the ways the doing actually gets done.

Little by little, Betty challenged the stories she had been telling herself. Slowly, she returned to well-being and peace. It's not that Betty stopped having goals or striving to succeed, but she related to her work and her identity in a completely different way. She moved from the fear of "Who will I be if I don't do X, Y, Z?" to trusting "I will still be, period, even if I don't do X, Y, Z."

WHAT IS THE SELF?

The self (or the identity) is made up of an experience of our five senses and our thoughts around the basic premise that my "I" is inherently real and separate from every other "I." This experience manifests in beliefs such as "I am this" and "I am not that," and thus the idea of a permanent, predictable, and reliable "self" is born.

In a famous and perplexing talk titled "Discourse on the Not Self," the Buddha addresses this idea of a permanent self by showing several monks how impermanent their feelings and thoughts are. Through a series of questions, Buddha points out that feelings come and go, thoughts come and go, body sensations come and go. None of them are permanent or enduring. Thus, if there is a self made up of these things, it can't be a permanent one.[1]

In addition, we think of our "I" as being in control. However, as we've discussed, our thoughts and feelings arise unbidden; that is, we don't control when they come into our awareness. Likewise, we don't really have control over our bodies. If we did, we would simply tell the body to lose weight or grow two inches and it would do it. Alas, we see the limits of the self.

Why can't we see what the self really is; that is, impermanent and not in control? Because we have an innate need to maintain permanence and create a way of appearing in control. We need others to see us as fixed, consistent, predictable beings. We want to be seen as beneficial and effective. Psychologist Anthony Greenwald coined the term *beneffectance* to describe this phenomenon.[2]

The need to belong to a tribe is an innate part of our wiring. It helped us survive for thousands of years. Imagine presenting yourself as indecisive and unreliable to everyone around you. Probably not the best way to make friends. However, if your friends are unpredictable and unreliable, you would want to show up similarly. Anyone who has attended junior high school understands this dilemma. We make ourselves fit in based on our environment, changing as necessary to do so. For example, we might start playing a sport or take up the same hobby as our friends. We are much less fixed than we like to think. As a human race, we are also fairly good at deluding ourselves about our own moral goodness, thinking we are above average in many different dimensions in life despite evidence to the contrary.

We all see ourselves a certain way and are reluctant to

change, even when that way creates a lot of suffering for ourselves and others, as it did for Betty. It takes great courage, an ability to pay attention, and a willingness to let go to begin to choose something different. This is the moment of waking up.

We all "play" in two reality planes: the ultimate, or inherently true, and the conventional. The ultimate refers to what we are moment by moment—what we give our attention to, our constantly shifting experience, our arising and receding thoughts and emotions. We are inherently impermanent. If we look for a permanent self or "I," we will not find it.

That being said, we interact with one another in the conventional plane. My impermanent "I" talks with your impermanent "I." In addition, when I stub my toe on the end of the bed, I definitely know that I exist. However, that doesn't mean the "I" is permanent. The pain in my toe will go away. In the conventional plane we appear to exist inherently, but we actually lack an inherent existence because we are constantly changing and influenced by the surrounding phenomenon. As Zen master Shunryu Suzuki said, "Of course the bird we see and hear exists. It exists, but what I mean by that may not be exactly what you mean."[3]

The conventional world is also the here and now, and it

involves the experience of sitting in a chair, driving to work, talking with friends, and so on. The constructs of time and money are part of the conventional world. Names are as well, so we don't refer to each other as "Hey, you!" Descriptions and names are convenient and conventional, but they aren't inherently real. Given the tangible, visible nature of the conventional world, it's easy to view it and ourselves as permanent and unchanging. This is one of the biggest myths we believe about the self.

When we think of our identity as fixed, we set ourselves up for suffering. We will experience situations that don't line up with our image. What happens then? What if I see myself as the person who works eighty hours a week and I come down with pneumonia that requires hospitalization? I will react. Fear will arise. We can also slip into self-condemnation and judgment. In a sense, our judgment is an act of identifying that makes the sense of self stronger. It's a self-fulfilling prophecy: the act of identifying with something (e.g., "I am this" or "I am not that") is an unconscious attempt to make the thing permanent. We are trying to make that aspect stay or go away. Our identity comes from the thing we identify with or not. For example, when anger arises, I might decide my anger is justified. I then become more attached to my anger and take the actions of an angry person. It can't be any other way. In that moment, I am identified with anger and can only take the actions of an angry person.

The opposite is also true. If I experience anger but don't become attached to it, I will not act like an angry person because I'm not an angry person. I am a person experiencing a momentary experience of sensations and thoughts that I would label as anger. It can't be any other way. If we identify with anger, fear, or judging, we are creating an identity around those things.

THE BODY

One aspect of the self is the body. We are heavily identified with our body. In fact, we believe we *are* our bodies. If something "goes wrong" with our body, we react because our well-being feels threatened at the core. We can challenge that reaction, however, if we remember nothing is permanent and we aren't in control. Like our thoughts and emotions, the body is always changing. Think about it: none of us have the same body we had when we were five. The ankle you sprained last year no longer hurts. The ache in your shoulder comes and goes, depending on the weather. The cells in your body completely die and recycle every twenty-four hours. The body and its sensations are constantly changing.

In relation to the way we identify with our body, consider this question: when does the body become a body? Is my body still a body if I cut off all my hair? What about my fingernails? What happens if I have my appendix or a kidney removed? When I was studying to become a physical therapist, we worked with cadavers (note: we didn't call them bodies). It wasn't too long into the semester before arms were removed from the torso and different bones and muscles were spread out across tables to better learn of their unique structures. As these parts were removed, was there a point at which the body ceased to be a body?

The point here is to see the limits of language and the way we identify with this thing we call the body. Our body is constantly changing. It is made up of various parts, many of which function without our conscious control—for example, breathing, heart pumping. If it was "my" body, it seems there should be a "me" controlling all aspects of it, but this is not the case. We don't need to believe this truth by blind faith. We can experience it by simply paying attention to the passing sensations and aspects of bodily function that are beyond our control.

Still, it's wise to take care of our bodies. We should eat well, exercise, and get regular checkups. The point of doing so, however, isn't to control the future. The body belongs to nature. It's going to do what it's going to do. You can run five miles a day and still catch the flu or have a heart attack. It's out of our control. The point of taking care of yourself is to give yourself the best experience now, in the present, and to live fully with the best energy we can access in any moment. Do what you can to help yourself enjoy the present and to bring more peace and joy to those around you.

Science has shown us the many benefits that can come from regular exercise, or whatever you call your rituals of moving well every day.[4] Walking your dog, going for a run, riding your bike, chasing your two-year-old—all of these and more count as movement. The point is to move the body regularly every day and to avoid becoming too sedentary. Find those activities you enjoy, and fully immerse yourself in the experience. For me, it's going for a run and walking my dog among the trees and flowers. The body and the mind—and the health of both—are interconnected. When we nurture the body, we feed the mind. We become more productive and learn faster too.

We also want to be aware of what we put into our bodies. We are intended to get pleasure from eating, as doing so ensures the survival of our bodies. Nevertheless, as with any other pleasure, identifying with the pleasure of eating can lead us to become attached to it. No one can out-exercise an unhealthy diet. Whereas the old prescription of "eat less, move more" seemed like good advice, it apparently hasn't solved our obesity epidemic. The emerging science on the effects of overdosing on sugar and refined carbohydrates show why we have gained more weight in the past fifty years despite the reality that we are consuming the same amount of calories within the same time period. "Rates of obesity, defined as having a body mass index of greater than 30, dramatically increased, starting almost exactly in 1977,"[5] around the time Americans started shifting to low-fat and high-carbohydrate diets.

We will all experience the vicissitudes of life, including health and illness. There is no escaping it. Aging, injuries, and health problems just happen. They are part of the is-ness of life, the such-ness of being a human on the planet. Taking care of the body and the mind are both necessary requirements for living our best life now.

THE VICISSITUDES OF LIFE

Everyone experiences the vicissitudes of life: pleasure and pain, praise and blame, gain and loss, fame and disrepute. We cannot control when or how these vicissitudes will arise, but experiencing these things—the preferred and nonpreferred—is one of life's few constants. Those things you are identified with are bound to change. You will not always experience success. You will not always be pain-free. Embrace this truth with an open hand and let go of the need to keep things a certain way. You will have more joy and well-being as a result.

When life shows up with its vicissitudes, we can get into a battle. If we're identified with having a certain status level or income and we experience a change in that level, we react. We resist what is actually occurring. We try to get things back to the way they were and sometimes find ourselves longing for the good ol' days or obsessively planning for the future. This is when we experience suffering. The problem isn't the thing that changed. It's our reaction to the change. And ultimately, we lose sight of the wisest actions that can only be taken in the present moment.

Our fearful reaction results from a fear of not knowing who we are in this new reality. If I've always been the rich person and I experience significant financial loss, I can no longer identify with money. But who am I without money? The opposite is also true. If I grew up in poverty and suddenly have money, I might not be able to accept the change.

We want to find security in that which is predictable and reliable. If we hang our security hat on things outside ourselves and believe them to be the ultimate reality, then when they change (which they will), we can find ourselves in the reactivity of fear, repeating the same patterns again and again to create the same old self. Only deep attention can allow us to see the pattern for what it is and keep us from repeating it.

Gaining a flexible sense of self starts with paying attention, as discussed in chapter 3. First, we need to notice when we slip into thinking the self is permanent. Notice when you start focusing on *my* project, *my* team, and *my* money. Notice when you start to justify yourself or feel judged by others. Both are evidence of trying to prop up or defend something you believe is inherently, constantly, permanently you. Second, we need to pay attention to where we get caught in the world of shoulds: life *should* be different, this *shouldn't* be happening to me, and so on.

Once we're paying attention and we recognize these ruminations, we don't have to convince ourselves of anything. We don't have to take anything by faith. Our direct observations of our moment-by-moment experience show us the truth that everything changes. There's no fancy footwork or mystical mind tricks. If we can simply train our attention to focus on the present, we will see that nothing is fixed or permanent—including the self. Then we can choose how to respond.

Psychologist and researcher Martin Seligman landed on a similar truth when he was studying optimistic versus pessimistic explanatory styles. Though he didn't talk about attachment or seeing the self as permanent, Seligman did describe two ways in which people respond to external events. Those with a pessimistic style tend to see nonpreferred events as permanent, pervasive, and personal. This style parallels closely with the idea of seeing the self as permanent. Those with an optimistic explanatory style, on the other hand, see nonpreferred events as impermanent, nonpervasive, and impersonal. This style relates closely to the ultimate truth of the impermanent nature of life. Interestingly, Seligman found an optimistic style creates greater levels of well-being as it pertains to health, success at work, and relationships.[6]

For example, if my boss sends me an angry email and I have an optimistic explanatory style, I might think to myself, "Wow. José seems really upset. He must be having a bad day. I wonder if something happened at home." I don't take his anger personally. I see that he must be having a bad day. I don't see the email as pervasive, or something that is going to affect my whole life. It's just one email. And I don't see it as permanent. I understand that there might be a single passing event in José's life that prompted his angry words. I know this one email does not mean all future emails will contain angry words. If I have a pessimistic explanatory style, however, I will take the angry words personally, and I will expect this to be José's permanent outlook toward me. I will view the email not as it pertains to a behavior but, instead, as a character assassination and something that will impact not just this moment at work, but all areas of my life (pervasive). In so doing, I cause my own suffering.

The truth is that unfortunate events happen. Angry emails happen. Messages of praise happen too. They are simply part of the vicissitudes of life. They are not permanent. When we pay attention, we see that our experience doesn't have the continuity we would like it to. It simply arises and passes. Knowing this essential truth, we can let go of striving to keep things the same. We can relax and let life unfold.

LETTING GO IS A SKILL

You can learn the skill of letting go of the self bit by bit. As mentioned, it's not some mystical practice for the chosen few sitting on a mountaintop. Everyone can learn to pay attention, separate fact from story, and consciously bring the attention back to transformational truths. Everyone can experience freedom, peace, and well-being. It's just a matter of collecting your attention long enough to see what you're thinking and feeling and how you're relating. Then the choices are in front of you. It's not anything you need to believe in. It's an experience. That being said, you do need to practice, which we'll discuss next.

A TRANSACTIONAL LOOK AT THE SELF

As we've said in each relationship chapter, learning about the transformational truths is not enough. We need to practice and apply these skills in our daily transactions.

TRANSACTING FROM FEAR

When we operate from fear, many patterns show up through our actions in relation to how we see ourselves. Two patterns will be mentioned here, as they are relevant to how we take action in the world and how we continue to create a false sense of "I" or "me."

Shoulding and Judging

If we don't accept that life changes, we will get stuck in shoulding and judging. For example, if I get laid off, I might think I shouldn't be laid off. The company should have laid off someone else. There are so many ways that we "should" ourselves and others based on the identity we have fixed in our mind: I should get the promotion. My team should do what I say. They should like working with me. I should be quieter.

Shoulding and judging yourself (and others) doesn't really contribute to our greatest well-being or the well-being of others. The reason is that shoulding and judging fight reality, or the deepest truth of what is happening right now. If I am experiencing anger and I start believing that I shouldn't be angry, I'm fighting the reality that I am experiencing anger. That's a little crazy, isn't it? When you start shoulding yourself, ask, "What is happening?" Anger is here right now. Giving yourself a moment to experience that reality allows you the freedom to see what wants to arise next. It's also worth remembering that shoulds and judgments are only thoughts. When we give them too much attention and become identified with them, we and those around us will suffer.

Consider this scenario. Great Aunt Mildred shows up at your house on Sunday morning. You open the door and say, "Aunt Mildred, you shouldn't be here!" She looks at you somewhat blankly and says, "But I am here." What would happen if you keep trying to tell her that she shouldn't be there when she's standing right in front of you? Fighting the reality of the moment induces suffering. When we're clinging to what we think should be and trying to control the impermanent, we have no freedom to see differently. We're stuck in that reactive loop.

Instead, we could simply accept that Aunt Mildred is there for a moment. We could allow what is occurring to occur and see what arises next. Perhaps we will realize we want to invite Aunt Mildred in for coffee, after all. Or maybe Aunt Mildred will decide that she just wanted to give a quick hello and be on her way. Or maybe you'll both stand at the door for a bit and chat.

Part of the reason we get upset with ourselves is we think we should be the self who _____ (fill the in the blank: never gets angry, never says the wrong thing, always acts selflessly, always turns projects in on time). We create this fixed identity of ourselves as the one who does this and the one who doesn't say that. When we don't do this or we do say that, we judge ourselves harshly. When we grasp the truth that we are not the fixed identity we create in our minds, we more readily realize that we often say and do many different things. We may need to become more skillful in some areas, and that's okay.

This also applies to others. Realize the people on your team don't have a fixed identity either. You may want them to be on time to every meeting and handle every difficult client with grace, but they won't. If you grasp this truth that no one has a fixed identity, you will stop shoulding and judging others as well. You will also be able to have true compassion.

Does this mean we're nihilistic or deterministic? No. You still need to take responsibility for unskillful words and actions. It also means that you can have a moment of grace with yourself regarding your unskillful moments.

Do we cease having expectations for ourselves and others? No. Expectations and goals are not the issue. It's how we relate to them. We will discuss goals at length in chapter 9.

Ambition

Ambition is what drove me to have no less than five different certifications at a time, while simultaneously taking on clinical research and more responsibility at work. It all stemmed from how I related to this idea of being a self, specifically, a fear of not being someone in the world, of not having enough power and status. It also came from thinking a future something would bring me happiness. I believed money—and the status and power it seemed to bring—was the means by which my external life could be changed for the better. I believed that one day, I would have it all. Without the degrees and certifications and job titles, I believed I wouldn't have the identity I needed to be happy. I also believed that if I didn't experience the status, power, and money, I would be doomed to a mundane existence, forever asking, "Is this all there is?"

When we're motivated by ambition, we try to amass all of sorts of things (for me it was these titles and degrees) to make ourselves look and feel a certain way and to create and preserve our identity, our sense of self. We're like a decorator crab, which roams about the aquarium stealing rocks and sticking them to its Velcro-like shell (I had a decorator crab in college, in case you were wondering). The decorator crab decorates itself for camouflage; we do it to preserve a certain image. Our actions are futile, however, because of the vicissitudes of life. Things are always changing, including who we are.

We all intuitively know that the quality of our life doesn't depend directly on what other people think of us or what type of car we own or what clothes we wear. Many of us have experienced the reality that we can amass the external fortunes of the world and still find ourselves fairly unhappy. As we've illustrated, our sense of well-being is greatly influenced by what we give our attention to. If we give our attention to the endless barrage of advertising that says a better body will make us happy, we may find ourselves endlessly chasing an idealized version of a leg or belly. If we give our attention to the thought that we aren't successful enough or aren't accomplishing enough in our lives, we will be consumed with an endless task list. We will work overtime to overcome that thought, even sacrificing relationships in the process, not recognizing that it is simply a thought and not reality. However, if we give our attention to impacting others in a helpful way and to believing we have value regardless of the things we own, we won't be pulled around by ambition, and we will make wiser choices.

TRANSACTING FROM TRUST

As we learn to choose trust over fear and become aware of how we interact with our daily lives, we experience a new way of being with ourselves. As our internal world undergoes its own transformation, it spills over into the external.

Equanimity

When we realize the impermanence of everything, we also gain balance and equanimity. Equanimity is the experience of seeing the big picture and, at the same time, being in it fully. In seeing the big picture, it isn't that we stand outside our lives, observing events like impartial spectators. Remaining aloof like this can suck the energy out of life and leave it feeling dry. Instead, we can stay in each experience, truly feel the anger or joy or disappointment, yet remain balanced because we know this too shall pass. If I know things won't always be as I expect, for example, I won't panic when someone shows up late. I won't berate my team when metrics go down in the third quarter. I can be at peace with myself and others and still take the necessary actions.

Conversely, I can also fully embrace the moments of joy and success in life. I can recognize that those, too, shall pass. I can appreciate them and let them go. If I am experiencing equanimity, I will not feel the need to attach myself to positive moments or to keep them going out of fear of losing them.

It's not that we don't care about timeliness and upward trends. We want the best for the company, our colleagues, and ourselves. But we are open to wisdom that acknowledges things don't have to happen in a certain way, at a certain time, or every time. We also know that we don't control much, if any, of what happens, including who we think we are. When we grasp the truth of impermanence and that our experience is created by what we give our attention to, our transactions with others improve. Our hearts and minds relax, and we can act with wisdom and compassion. We realize there's nothing we need from the outside world, per se, and yet, there's so much we can give in the way of generosity and kindness. We can make a choice to learn and bring our best selves to the situation and circumstance. That's real power.

Generosity

From the Buddhist perspective, the first character quality one should cultivate is generosity. This is considered the first quality of an awakened mind. While many of us can find ourselves willing to sit and meditate, we often skip over this powerful practice that can significantly contribute to our ability to pay attention and experience calm. Generosity allows us to experience a deeper sense of peace and plays a significant role in learning to let go willingly, especially of the self.

The act of generosity can be lived in many different ways. We can be generous with our patience with others and ourselves, generous with our time, and generous with our money. The key is to give freely, without expectation of return and without obligation. True generosity involves a letting go without anticipation. This letting go has great power in working with our identities, which want so much to hang on.

Many people who have created large fortunes do actually give of those fortunes. Interestingly, though, this generosity only seems to occur once they have everything they *believe* they will need. This is how greed works: "I will be generous, but only when I am certain I have everything I need." Or "I will be generous, once I am certain I am in control of how things will turn out." This isn't generosity that affords us the gift of letting go. Nevertheless, we can begin here, right where we are.

Generosity impacts the one who is giving and correlates strongly with psychological health and well-being. Research on generosity demonstrates that those who volunteer report a greater quality of life, those who offer help to others freely have a greater sense of vitality, and that generosity in the workplace is associated with reducing burnout. All three of these scenarios demonstrate a generosity of time. In intimate relationships, generosity is associated with more contentment and longevity of the relationship.[7]

In addition, we can practice generosity with ourselves. If we understand generosity as a letting go, we can be generous with ourselves and let go of painful states like frustration and envy when they arise. Just as we might encourage a friend to let go, knowing he will not feel good by keeping jealousy or anger around, we can be generous with ourselves and release those painful feelings. We practice generosity to ourselves by letting go of our suffering.

We also are generous with ourselves when we acknowledge the skillful choices we've made that have contributed to the benefit of others, instead of focusing on the choices that have not. By seeing the truth of how our generous nature benefits all beings, we let go of erroneous beliefs in the me who thinks the only way to be happy and at peace is to get mine.

STRENGTHS

One way to show generosity is by using our strengths to support others. Strengths can be seen as the gifts we've been given, like a sense of humor or the ability to edit grammar and writing. We can choose to be generous with these gifts and use them to benefit others.

Using our strengths also benefits us. When we do what we do best, we feel energized and alive. Thus, engaging in work that employs our strengths is a way of being generous with ourselves too.

However, using our strengths doesn't give us license to continue exhibiting negative behaviors such as constantly interrupting customers on the phone or yelling at coworkers. It also doesn't mean we use our strengths with blind abandon. We must exercise wisdom. For example, even though a sense of humor is a strength, using it in the middle of an organization-wide meeting about sexual harassment in the office may not be a skillful choice.

To understand more about using your strengths and to discover your own, go to www.viacharacter.org.

Compassion

Compassion comes from the true realization that we are all vulnerable to reactivity and the vicissitudes of life. Everyone experiences pain and loss, joy and success. Everyone chooses unskillful words and shows up late. Everyone creates their own suffering from time to time. There's no separation between us; none of us gets out alive. We all have the same ultimate hopes, dreams, and aspirations. We all want to feel appreciated, engage in meaningful work, and get a good night's sleep. Knowing this, our decisions regarding our business and our team are made from wisdom and compassion.

The story of the mustard seed from the time of the Buddha illustrates our human connection and shows the need for compassion with self and others. In the parable, a woman named Kisa Gotami had lost her young son. Grief-stricken, she was unwilling to accept his death and carried him from town to town, lamenting and begging people to bring him back to life. Eventually, one of the townspeople suggested she go to the Buddha. Perhaps he could offer a solution. Kisa went to the Buddha, carrying her deceased son, and begged for a cure. The Buddha instructed her to go back to her village and collect mustard seeds from every household that had not been touched by death. Once she brought him these mustard seeds, he would provide a solution for her. So, Kisa returned to her village and began asking for mustard seeds.

She found many households had mustard seeds, but not one household was untouched by death. Each home had lost a loved one. Upon recognizing this truth, Kisa spoke these words to her deceased son: "No village law, no market town, no law of a single house is this. Of all the world and all the worlds of gods, this only is the Law, that all things are impermanent."[8]

While this story directly illustrates the ultimate reality of death and, thus, impermanence, it also shows the interconnectedness of all humans in the conventional here and now. Remembering this truth will open us to deeper compassion and wisdom for ourselves and all beings.

One note about compassion: knowing I don't have a fixed self doesn't mean I let people walk all over me. That's idiot compassion. Letting people do whatever they want to me isn't kind to myself or others. Compassion does mean that I go into conversations more open and curious about what is actually happening. I become more interested in how we can all get our needs met. If I'm wisely compassionate, I want to explore how our organization can make money *and* take care of the planet. Life is no longer either-or.

The Art of Being Human

Ultimately, the self is an awareness. What we choose to let into our awareness—rather, what we choose to give our attention to—determines the quality of our experience. It cannot be any other way.

Although the self is not a permanent, tangible entity, in the conventional world, we still interact with tangible humans, and we do well when we keep our heart engaged on our greatest intentions—on the internal, inherent truths, not only our external, conventional circumstances. The practice of living hinges on how much attention we give to making changes in the external world in the hopes that we will be happier the next day, versus working with our internal experience and attention to experience in our life fully right now with wisdom and compassion. As we've seen, some changes in the external parts of our lives may be of great benefit to our well-being. However, the world is impermanent and the brand-new pair of shoes I'm enjoying now will certainly become torn, worn out, and unwearable in due time. If I am attached to them as a fixed expression of who I am, I will certainly suffer.

Nonetheless, I do enjoy my shoes, and I have intentions for this life. There is this book to write, and when I put on my orange tennis shoes, I find the writing and the wearing of my shoes enjoyable. I am fully immersed in both and give my full attention to the way my shoes feel on my feet and the way their orange color looks in the morning sunlight. I fully feel the smack of the keys on the keyboard and the way the words seem to rise up out of nowhere on the screen. I am absorbed in the moment. There is nowhere else to be and nothing else to do. When I tie my shoes, I am fully aware that I am tying my shoes. When I am typing on the computer, I am fully aware that I am typing on the computer. This is the full enjoyment of living and the art of being human: being in the conventional world and fully realizing the ultimate truths.

If we only understand logically that there is no fixed self, then what does it matter how any of us act? We can do whatever we want, right? No, that's not how it works best. If you look at ancient Eastern writings, the Ten Commandments, and many of the world's contemplative traditions and philosophies, they all say similar things. Be decent human beings. Be kind to each other. Don't steal. Don't kill. Don't take your neighbor's wife. This, too, is the art of being human: engaging with ourselves, with the things we enjoy in the world, and with others in a mutually beneficial way. As well, when we act in accordance with our best virtues and with our fullest attention to the day-to-day moments of our lives, we are more likely to create our best experience, which in turn supports others to do the same.

Martin Seligman writes,

> We have invented myriad shortcuts to good feelings. Drugs, chocolate, loveless sex, shopping, television are all examples. Positive emotions, alienated from the exercise of character, lead to emptiness, to inauthenticity, to depression. The positive feeling that arises from the exercise of strength and virtues, rather than shortcuts, is authentic. Strengths and virtues are characteristics that bring about good feelings, and gratification.[9]

I would add that acting in alignment with our virtues and strengths also lets us get a good night's sleep.

The discussion of our relationship with the self is deliberately placed in the middle of the other four relationships. The way we relate to our identity impacts all other relationships. Letting go of the idea of a fixed, permanent self is central to our personal and professional experience of peace and well-being, as is allowing ourselves to become fully involved in life. Since what we give our attention to determines the quality of our experience, and since we cannot control the external vicissitudes of life, we do well to tend to this internal relationship.

This kind of mindfulness is not reserved for the chosen few. Betty, the Every Leader, learned it, and so can you. Doing so will improve several relationships, especially your relationship with other humans.

EXERCISE: PRACTICE OF SELF-COMPASSION

Goal: One of the ways we get caught up in the self is through self-judgment. We identify with the self and believe it's a fixed entity, then we judge and criticize it. Ironically, this self-condemnation creates a stronger sense of self. This exercise offers ways to combat this tendency through self-compassion, a key transformational skill.[10]

Process:

1. *Be kind to yourself.* Meet yourself the way you would a friend. Be understanding and gentle toward yourself when you fail or when something doesn't turn out as you'd hoped. Take a moment right now to consider one thought you've had that arises as a self-judgment or criticism. How would you respond to a friend who shared this thought with you? Would you tell him to believe it? How can you respond to this thought? Do you tell yourself to believe

it? What would happen if you stopped believing it? What would happen if you gave it very little of your attention? What could you put your attention on instead that would be more aligned with your virtues and strengths?

2. *See our common humanity.* Recognize that you're not as separate from others as you think. We all make mistakes, say the wrong thing, suffer disappointment, and experience pain. Remind yourself that you are not the only one in the history of the world to ever experience what you are experiencing. Do you know someone who has experienced the same difficulties of self-judgments? Or maybe you've read about or listened to a podcast by someone with a similar experience. Is this judgment that arises about yourself unique? How might you see others who have this same thought arise?

3. *Practice mindfulness.* Observe your experience without judgment and criticism. You don't have to ignore what's going on, but you also don't have to fight against it or try to hold on to something else. If you're really stuck, use a meditation like the RAIN Meditation described in chapter 4. If you would like to practice a meditation on self-compassion, please visit www.wakingupaleader.com.

CHAPTER 8

FRIENDSHIPS

"Friendship is a mirror to presence and a testament to forgiveness."

—DAVID WHYTE

This may seem odd, but we're going to open this friendship chapter by talking about suicide.

In his book *Homo Deus: A Brief History of Tomorrow*, Yuval Noah Harari has some interesting statistics on causes of death among humans. He notes that:

> ...in 2012 about 56 million people died throughout the world; 620,000 of them died due to human violence (war killed 120,000 people and crime killed another 500,000). In contrast, 800,000 committed suicide. For the first time in history, more people are committing suicide than are being killed by soldiers, terrorists and criminals combined.[1]

(It should also be noted that 1.5 million died of diabetes, hence the importance of what we eat, as stated earlier.)[2]

In his book *How to Change Your Mind*, Michael Pollan cites the rising rates of depression and suicide as a symptom of being stuck in isolation. This stuck condition, both as individuals and a culture, is the reason we need to change our minds.[3] Research estimates that in the United States alone, 3.4 percent of the population, or eight million Americans, suffer from some form of serious psychological distress.[4] And suicide is rising alarmingly. According to the CDC, death by suicide has increased by 25 percent since 1999, becoming the second greatest cause of death in people fifteen to thirty-four years of age.[5]

Why are we seeing this drastic increase in suicide? What is the root issue? As Pollan suggests, I believe it's a widespread lack of connection, first to oneself and then to others.[6] For reasons we'll discuss, people are becoming increasingly isolated, and humans were not meant to function that way. The research also tells us that having connections with people we call friends supports our physical health, protects us from disease (even more than avoiding smoking), and, for the most part, allows us to experience greater levels of positive emotion and happiness.[7]

Since many of us spend a great deal of time and energy at

work, and since belonging is important to our psychological health, it makes sense to consider our relationships at work as a vital part of our well-being. This chapter dives into the importance of human connection, what keeps us from connecting, and ways to form high-quality friendships, particularly in the workplace.

A TRANSFORMATIONAL LOOK AT FRIENDSHIP

As we leave the dot of fear that keeps us chained to patterns of relating to time, money, and the self, it only makes sense to also consider how we relate to other people. This is the big one for most of us. As people and leaders, we require connection and friends. As the Beatles said, "I get by with a little help from my friends." It's true for us all.

WHAT IS FRIENDSHIP?

British psychologist and psychiatrist John Bowlby studied the impacts of disrupted relationships between mother and child, particularly the detrimental impacts on child development when these relationships weren't intact. He began working with children during the early stages of World War II, many of whom were evacuated from London and separated from their families due to air raids. These children exhibited behavioral patterns such as lethargy and difficulty connecting with others, as well as more disturbing behaviors such as banging their heads against the wall. However, if these children had some contact with their mothers, they were suddenly able to connect with others in the orphanage and their behaviors of withdrawal and anger subsided. Bowlby concluded that even though the children were given food and shelter, they developed psychological issues because they didn't have a connection with a caring source.[8]

Although Bowlby's work primarily concerned the impact of familial relationships, attachment also seems like the foundation for a definition of friendship. I would add that this connectedness with those we call friends is grounded on curiosity, trust, and forgiveness.

Around the same time that Bowlby was studying children, Harry Harlow was studying a similar theory of attachment in rhesus monkeys. After the mothers gave birth, Harlow took the babies away. The babies were given food and were kept warm, but they developed destructive behaviors similar to the children in the orphanages. Then Harlow put a soft diaper on a metal statue that was supposed to look like a mother monkey. He put the statue into the cage and found the babies clung to it. He also put a bottle on some statues with the soft diaper and on some without. The monkeys went to the statue with the bottle *and* the diaper every time. He concluded the monkeys wanted to feel a connection to something soft and nurturing, similar to what they may have had with their mother figure.[9]

Both studies led to the development of attachment theory, which says that normal human development requires more than money, food, and shelter. We require connection with other human beings. My definition of friendship is based on this theory. Even after we become adults, we still require connection with others. This is where friends and family play a vital role in our lives. As well, considering how much energy we put into our work and the fact that relationships occur there, too, it is worth creating thriving friendships in our work lives as well as out.

WHAT FRIENDSHIP ISN'T

When I was in the midst of my striving years, piling up degrees, certifications, and work responsibilities, I had a lot of business relationships and acquaintances. I took doctors out to dinner, attended sporting events with potential clients, and hung out with work-related folks. But these activities did not a friendship make. I didn't have true connections with those people. We talked about the weather and work, but we didn't delve into really meaningful topics like our personal relationships or what kept us up at night. Essentially, we skated over vulnerability, and the friendship foundations of curiosity, trust, and forgiveness didn't come into play. In my ambition and attempts to keep my identity intact, I became disconnected from myself, so I certainly wasn't connected with those around me.

This is a common scenario among professionals today. We exist in isolated silos, pursuing our own thing and bouncing through life separated from one another. Also, there is the quest to remain revered, respected, and seen as someone who has it all together. We want to maintain an identity of "the boss." The problem is that this life ultimately leads to being alone, depressed, and worse, as the suicide statistics indicate.

The nonmindful business culture in the United States values ambition and getting things done more than it values human life or spending time helping another person. Here's the real root: most of our interactions with people in organizations involve narrow agendas that don't operate at a human level of connection.

We have to be willing to let go of our agendas. True friendship can never operate when I have an agenda for how you should be or what you should be doing. This is a tricky balance for leaders who need to set expectations and get results from their teams. We also have to stop trying to get others to see us in a certain way. This is related to letting go of our sense of a fixed identity.

In organizations, we have assigned roles: director of magical mountaintops, vice president of fairies and goblins. On top of that, however, we assign people roles in our personal movie. We designate the ways people should show up; that is, the ways people should behave toward us. Then we end up disappointed because no one shows up the way we think they should. Assigning roles isn't friendship. That's a world of judging and comparing. When we have expectations like this, we end up being alone. Therefore, friendship is based not on perfection but instead upon being present with each other in each moment, as best we can.

FORGIVENESS

Over time, I have discovered the deep foundation of friendship is a path of forgiveness, but not always in the way we traditionally think of forgiving. We've been taught that forgiveness means letting someone off the hook for something they did wrong to us. I've found that forgiveness goes much deeper than that. It means forgiving both parties for the misunderstanding we both created. It seems that people will disappoint us fairly regularly. However, I've found that I typically have my part in the misunderstanding too. If we're willing to look closely at situations that arise between ourselves and others, we can almost always find expectations that were unspoken and, subsequently, unmet. We unconsciously put people into the characters we want them to play in our lives, and when the lights go up, we expect them to hit their mark. Often, they do not and, as often, not through any fault of their own. If I understand how it works for me—that I have untrue thoughts, that I try to prop up a fixed identity, that I can exhibit greed out of fear—I can understand that it's the same for others and have compassion when they don't act as I think they should.

Author Byron Katie, best known for her method of self-inquiry known as "The Work," offers a radical way of seeing our misunderstandings with others. During an in-person retreat, someone once asked her if, based on her view of the world, anyone is ever guilty of anything. She said, "No. If you thought and believed the way that person did, you would do the exact same thing." Katie was held up at gunpoint one time. She gave the guy her purse and said, "You obviously need this more than I do." The guy was dumbfounded and didn't bother her any-more. When asked how she could do that, Katie said, "He believes something. There's something in his mind telling him he needed to do that. If I believed what he does, I would do the exact same thing." This deep understanding through compassion and being in touch with reality is a way to true peace and clarity.

That being said, forgiveness does not mean we condone or approve of everything someone has done or said. We can take responsibility for expressing our needs, making requests, and setting clear boundaries. And we may find we need to separate ourselves from people who don't heed our requests or respect our boundaries. At the same time, however, we can't hang on to the wish that someone had acted differently in the past or will in the future. Doing so only adds the second arrow to an already challenging moment.

Forgiveness is never about the other person. It is always about our own internal work, learning to be with the reality of what has occurred. Wisdom and compassion allow us to see the past for what it really is. This thing occurred, and now it's no longer occurring. We are left with our feelings and thoughts about the occurrence and resolving our relationship to the situation in a way that brings us clarity and peace. That said, we are all in different stages of forgiveness. People who have suffered trauma may be in the very beginning stage. I'm not advocating that someone once-and-for-all forgive someone. We each have to come to forgiveness in stages and in our own way. Nevertheless, when it comes to maintaining long-term friendships and relationships with others, we will find that our ability to forgive them, and ourselves, is a key practice.

CONNECTION VERSUS ISOLATION

Given that we spend a majority of our time with people

at work, it is wise to create connections and friendships in our organizations. Contrary to the way we sometimes act, our colleagues are not simply a means to an end. Connections at work improve the well-being and vitality of all concerned. We need to learn to take a genuine interest in people because they're people, not because we're trying to get something from them.

At the root of our lack of connection, isolation, and the increasing suicide rates is a sense that we are separate from each other. When we believe in a fixed identity, life's hardships feel unique and personal. We cannot see that as humans, we're all in this together, experiencing the same trials and tribulations. Our culture promotes ambition and individualism, and businesses do too. That's what promotions are all about. A promotion says I am better than and different from you because I have a bigger title. I'm up here, and you're down there. The promotions and titles in and of themselves aren't the problem. How we relate to them, however, and the power we give them, can be, if we aren't awake.

One CFO I worked with had the opportunity to have a thirty-minute, once-a-month team coaching meeting. The goal would be to touch base, give individual updates on their emotional and mental energy, and focus on specific behaviors to bring them together as a team. In other words, to connect with each other. The CFO emailed me and said, "Although I find this incredibly vital, we are so busy that we don't have time for these meetings." What kind of connection do you think this CFO has with his team? What kind of connection do the team members have with each other? Probably not much. When we don't emphasize connection (and instead get caught up in time, money, and ambition), people become cogs in the wheel, worker bees, a means to an end. This lack of connection can lead to isolation, loneliness, and a lack of fulfillment.

WHY ARE FRIENDSHIPS IMPORTANT?

Up until now, we've focused a great deal on our own individual mindfulness and how to work with all of these parts of ourselves while we are transacting with others. Here we get to the other part of the equation of having a fulfilled life: the importance of other people. Without a doubt, other people can bring us the most joy and also the most heartache. Nevertheless, we require other people. Optimal functioning at work and in life requires three things: positive emotion, positive relationships, and positive meaning.[10] We want to feel like we're contributing to something greater than ourselves. This typically involves having an impact on other people and knowing that we're connecting to those around us in a positive way, both of which result in a good dose of positive emotion for all involved.

As discussed earlier, we need a balance of getting rid of the bad stuff and adding in the good stuff. Think of it this way: if a house catches on fire, we call the fire department to put it out. In a sense, we've eliminated the bad. But we don't have a thriving house at that point. We still need to rebuild the foyer, repair the roof, and so on. We don't automatically enjoy the positive when we remove the negative. We have to make a conscious choice to add, repair, and enhance.

One way we add to our lives is through friends and connection at work. Yes, we can have a house and food and our basic needs met. We can construct our day-to-day lives so they are relatively safe. But these actions don't ensure the full benefits we can get from helping other people and developing connected relationships along the way.

A TRANSACTIONAL LOOK AT FRIENDSHIP

If we want to be creative in this world, we need to feel safe with others. When we innovate and try new things, we're going to make mistakes. There will be times when our actions are not skillful. We're going to say something that rubs a colleague the wrong way. We're going to forget to give the report to the manager who requested it. We're going to say we'll be home at a certain time and then show up late. That's just part of being human.

When we've built the transformational connections, we can more skillfully manage the ups and downs of transacting with one another.

TRANSACTING FROM FEAR

Relationships with others can be one of the richest aspects of our lives, bringing us much joy. However, they can also bring us much suffering when fear arises. Next, we discuss some of the ways in which fear shows up in our relationships, both in and out of work.

Comparing, Fixing, and Judging

Comparing, fixing, and judging keep us from connecting with others. The untrained mind is fairly skilled at these three activities. In the workplace and in life, we compare ourselves to those around us and then we decide which one of us is better. For example, we decide whose call we'll return based on the imaginary hierarchy of importance we've created in our own mind. We do this because we are unconsciously trying to maintain that supposedly fixed identity.

As soon as we compare, we decide we need to fix something about ourselves or the other person. We do this so that we can measure up or so that the other person can look better, which will make us look better. For example, if one of my direct reports makes a mistake and everyone finds out about it, I want to correct it immediately or pass the buck because I don't want to look bad.

At the same time we're comparing and fixing, we're forming judgments around the comparisons. The judgments know no bounds. We think they should have known better, they should do better, they should be better—any version will do.

Comparing, fixing, and judging happen simultaneously and unconsciously. In our minds, it might sound like "They need to be different than they are. They shouldn't be like that. They should be more like this." The should-ing and judging we talked about in regard to the self also comes into play in our relationships with others.

As a leader, part of your responsibility may be evaluating people's behavior. If you have three people up for a promotion and one position, you have to compare the individuals and decide who is best for the job. You need to use discernment and skillful action in choosing. The critical difference between making an evaluation about behavior and comparing, fixing, and judging that stymies connection is that the latter happens on autopilot and carries a certain level of fear—fear of being wrong or of wanting to control everyone's reaction.

To avoid slipping into automatic reactivity, we need to

pay attention. We need to be aware of how we're relating to our teammates so that we don't slip into comparing, fixing, and judging and thereby create separation. When we need to give reviews, we do so from a place of trust, with our greatest intention to help the team or employee, not to avoid conflict or prop up a certain identity.

Seeing People as Objects

We sometimes view people as being a glass we can see through. We think we know everything about them. There's nothing new for us to know about their personality or capabilities. In other words, we view them as static, unchanging things. Then we *is* them. We tell ourselves that "Tim *is* like that" or "Stacey *is* like this." We don't see how they are always changing right in front of us.

If we view people at static objects, we won't be curious to know more. A key part of friendship is curiosity, and curiosity is linked to appreciation and caring. It drives us to see the uniqueness and nuance in the most mundane things. If you've worked with someone for a while, you might think you've reached the end of what you can know about her. Not true. You've simply stopped being curious and appreciative.

I've reliably had the experience of teams coming together for a group coaching session and at the end express how they had no idea what had been happening for each other, in and out of work. In these sessions, things shared would range from a recent cancer diagnosis to a spouse's struggle with alcoholism to a difficult family situation in which a child had run away from home. We often cannot see each other's struggles and imagine that if we keep our own hidden, we can protect our fragile identities, but instead, we simply suffer the loss of connection. What also reliably happens in these sessions is that through this level of vulnerability and sharing, people become closer and find greater capacity for friendship.

Tribalism

Another roadblock to connection is tribalism, or seeing everything inside our border as "us" and everything outside our border as "not us." We tend to relate to people as either of our tribe or not of our tribe, forgetting that we are all human.

According to Michael Pollan, objectifying people comes out of tribalism.[11] In other words, we see people who are not of us as objects, as a means to our end, and we only interact with those "outsiders" so we can get something from them. Such interactions do not foster friendship.

When we function in this tribalistic mentality, we focus on perceived differences rather than our true human similarities. In the workplace, tribalism can cause leaders to overlook what they have in common with individual contributors, managers in other departments, and "competitors" in other companies. It creates an us-versus-them mentality that impedes friendship, collaboration, and a cohesive culture.

Famous manager Michael Scott of the television show *The Office* played this tribalism dynamic in the way he created ongoing battles between the Scranton branch and corporate. Scott thought he was bolstering team spirit at Scranton. In reality, he was fostering drama, tension, and a lack of connection (although it makes for great comedy). I've seen organizations in which the investment team is perpetually at odds with the compliance team and marketing is always battling sales. As a result, people become increasingly constricted in their connections with other people. And the more limited our connections, the more isolated and alone we become.

TRANSACTING FROM TRUST

How do we create high-quality friendships, and what does it mean to do so from trust at work? According to researchers, building high-quality connections doesn't have to take years, days, or even hours. In her study of the workplace, Jane Dutton presents four ways of creating connection that can bring us closer in a relatively short time: task enabling, respectful engagement, trust, and play.[12] To these four I add a fifth from Shelly Gable known as active constructive responding, or appreciative joy from the Buddhist perspective.

Task Enabling

One way to create a connection with people at work is to help people when they need it. Someone might need information to finish a report or assistance in using a new computer program. Simply offering our assistance when we can is all it takes. Even handing someone a stapler when they don't have one nearby begins the process of supporting others to get their work done. To this end, a great question for leaders to ask themselves is "What is the one thing my team needs me to do for them today?"

Respectful Engagement

Another interaction with positive returns is respectful engagement. When someone shares an idea, acknowledge it. Respond with "yes, and" rather than "no, but" or "yeah, but." For example, after someone makes a suggestion, you can say, "Yes, and we can build on it this way." This is especially important in group settings. Through respectful engagement we can show compassion and understanding of what it takes for people to voice their thoughts and suggestions in a room of people, especially when the boss is sitting in. Even if you are completely at ease talking in front of a group, remember that it can be quite nerve-racking for others. By consistently responding with "yes, and," you can start to create a safe space for sharing ideas.

When someone makes a suggestion or shares a thought, it isn't necessary to be first to evaluate it. Respectful engagement is first the act of acknowledging the person and the fact they have spoken words into the room. This is also the foundation for building psychological safety. Individuals learn they can be heard and speak even if their ideas aren't always the first ones used. After they share, ideas can be built upon.

If you're the type of leader who readily shares first, try waiting until others have spoken. Give your team space to talk and not feel like they're competing with you. This is another aspect of respectful engagement.

Trust

In conversations with your team, let them know that you believe they can be successful at what they're doing. If you're constantly saying things like "I don't know if you're going to be able to do this" or "This is going to be really hard, and I'm not sure if we're up for it," your team is likely to become discouraged. They won't feel your support or connection. However, if you say things like "You got this" and "You might need a little more information, but I know you can handle this," you are communicating trust in their abilities, which will encourage connection. Of course, this doesn't mean blind optimism when things aren't going well or simply dumping tasks on individuals who clearly aren't capable of handling them. It does mean instilling a sense of confidence in those around you.

Play

Think about your friends outside of work. You get together and participate in activities you all enjoy. Bring the same philosophy into the office. In his book *Play: How It Shapes the Brain, Opens the Imagination, and Invigorates the Soul*, Stuart Brown discusses the different ways that we play at work and the many different types of play we can employ. This ability to take our work sincerely and yet play and make it engaging for ourselves and others is also part of how we create deep absorption for ourselves and others as well.[13] Playing practical jokes, telling funny stories, and kidding around in meetings are all examples of play with colleagues. This kind of play can enhance connection and build friendships at work.

There is one particular type of play, however, that can become unhelpful: play that occurs at the expense of another person. Jokes are great, but if those jokes are intended to zing a specific person with sarcasm, hold off on that approach. This toxic approach will have deleterious effects over time.

Active Constructive Responding and Appreciative Joy

Shelly Gable and her team offer another powerful means of creating connections at work and with those we might like to call friends: sharing in another's joy and success. This involves being actively constructive in how we respond to others' good news. According to Gable, the way we respond to people's good news matters even more than how we respond to their bad news. She determined that when someone shares their great news, there are four ways in which we could respond:[14]

1. Passive destructive. When someone shares good news, the listener doesn't say anything. The listener makes no comment or makes a comment that's turned around to the listener, for example, "Yeah, I did something like that once too" or "Oh yeah, Bob got that last year."

2. Active destructive. When someone shares good news, the listener quashes joy with a demeaning response. For example, "You guys, I have good news! I'm pregnant!" "Wow. Kiss your social life good-bye." Or "Hey, Samuel. I just got a promotion!" "Really? Are you sure you can handle the workload?"

3. Passive constructive. This response reveals low energy and little connection beyond the words spoken, for example, "Hey, we just closed the big real estate deal!" "Good job. Good for you."

4. Active constructive. This response to someone's good news is characterized by enthusiasm and authentic interest in the person's experience with their newest accomplishment. This involves asking the person specific questions about the ways they accomplished it and how they feel now that they have it. It supports a person in savoring the experience as well. For example, "Wow, I just hit my biggest sales quota ever." "Congratulations! How does it feel? What do you think were the biggest things you did that helped that happen? Will you do anything special to celebrate?"

What Gable describes as active constructive relates closely to appreciative joy from the Buddhist perspective. It is considered the antidote to the judging and comparing mind and envy.

Appreciative joy involves celebrating the positive events in people's lives. To show this kind of support, we must let go of comparison, judging, and all the other hindrances to connection, especially envy. As mentioned, when we unhook ourselves from expectations and agendas surrounding the self as well as others, we can fully enjoy another person's accomplishments because we know they don't take anything away from our own.

When we respond positively to others' good news, not only do they have positive emotion, but we enjoy a big dose of positive emotion too. This joint experience of joy and celebration creates connections. Knowing someone is going to celebrate your achievements and accomplishments with you is powerful.

We were meant to live in community and in connection with others, even at work. Tribalism, ambition, agendas, and viewing people as objects hinder connection and leave us feeling isolated and alone. In the extreme, lack of connection leads to depression and may be one of the greatest contributors to the growing rate of suicide.

Connection with others can also help us deal with the unknown, which is the last key relationship.

EXERCISE: THE CURIOSITY INTERVIEW

Lesson: Sourcing curiosity with others and in our relationships is a foundational practice in mindfulness and in creating connection.

Process: Take a moment to consider someone who is important to you, someone you might have a relatively good relationship with already. Now, consider what particular strengths and virtues you see in this person. You may think about a few specific interactions you've had with her or interactions you've seen her have with others.

Next, consider how this person may have learned these skills or come to possess these strengths or virtues. Did she learn them from a parent or caregiver? Who were some of the strong influences in her life? How have these attributes supported this person in life?

Let this person know you would like to grab coffee. When you meet, share some of your positive observations, ask questions, and be open to what you may discover through the conversation. This is what I call the Curiosity Interview. Afterward, ask yourself if you feel more connected to the person after grabbing coffee.

You can find out more about the Curiosity Interview and also how to conduct positive introductions with your team at www.wakingupaleader.com.

CHAPTER 9

THE UNKNOWN

"One is never afraid of the unknown; one is afraid of the known coming to an end."

—JIDDU KRISHNAMURTI

"The least revered sentence in the English language is 'I don't know.'"

—DAPHNE SCOTT

A man was talking to the Buddha, very concerned about the many things that hadn't been resolved in the world. Before listening to the Buddha's wisdom and before beginning a practice of meditation and mindfulness, the man needed to know how these issues would be fixed and needed to figure things out.

The Buddha replied,

It's as if a man were wounded with an arrow thickly smeared with poison. His friends and companions, kinsmen and relatives provided him with a surgeon. And the man would say, "I won't have this arrow removed until I know whether the man who wounded me was a noble warrior, a priest, a merchant, or a worker." He would say, "I won't have this arrow removed until I know the given name and clan name of the man who wounded me. Until I know whether he was tall, medium, or short, until I know whether he was dark, ruddy brown, or golden colored. Until I know his home village, town, or city. Until I know whether the bow with which I was wounded was a longbow or a crossbow. Until I know whether the bowstring with which I was wounded was fiber, bamboo thread, sinew, hemp, or bark. Until I know whether the shaft with which I was wounded was wild or cultivated. Until I know whether the feathers of the shaft with which I was wounded were those of a vulture, a stork, a hawk, a peacock, or another bird. Until I know whether the shaft with which I was wounded was bound with the sinew of an ox, a water buffalo, a lanyear or a monkey." He would say, "I won't have this arrow removed until I know whether the shaft with which I was wounded was that of a common arrow, a curved arrow, a barbed or captoothed, or an oleander arrow." The man would die, and those things would still remain unknown to him.[1]

In business and in life, we spend so much time behaving as the wounded man in this story. We won't do anything until we know. We try to figure out all the possibilities, but our efforts end up being an exercise in futility. Planning in and of itself isn't bad, nor is asking wise questions and listening to our own experience. It is helpful to plan our schedule and organize our life. The problem is we get so caught up in this type of thinking and way of being that we lose sight of our deepest truths and instead search aimlessly for that one thing that will bring us certain success. A certain level of prospection, or anticipating the future, is helpful. However, too much prospection can disrupt our emotions, sap our motivation, and lead to depression and stress.

The key is learning to be okay with not knowing and discovering for ourselves what is true in our experience. From this place of wisdom, we can effectively engage in goal setting and planning.

A TRANSFORMATIONAL LOOK AT THE UNKNOWN

An old farmer had worked his crops for many years. One day, his horse ran off. Upon hearing the news, the neighbors came to visit and said, "Oh, that's such bad luck that your horse ran off."

The farmer replied, "Well, maybe."

The next morning the horse came back and brought three

wild horses with it. The neighbors came over and said, "You just got three new horses. How wonderful!"

The farmer replied, "Well, maybe."

The next day the farmer's son tried to ride one of the wild horses. The son was thrown off and broke his leg. The neighbors came over and said, "Oh, we heard your son broke his leg. That's horrible!"

The farmer replied, "Well, maybe."

The following day military officials knocked on the farmer's door. They were drafting all eligible young men in the village. Since the young man had a broken leg, he wasn't drafted and sent off to war. The neighbors came over and said, "Wow! You're so lucky that your son had a broken leg."

The farmer replied, "Well, maybe."[2]

This story illustrates the transformational mindset we want to have in relation to the unknown: complete openness to whatever the future brings. The farmer responded to life's events with equanimity and perspective. He accepted reality, but he also understood that he didn't know what each event meant for the future and thus was not unnecessarily bereft or overjoyed at each piece of news.

WHAT IS THE UNKNOWN?

The unknown is the space between what we think we know in the present and how reality actually shows up in the next moment. This chapter is about how we relate to that space.

As humans, we have an innate desire to survive and feel safe. As a result, nothing is more perplexing to us than recognizing that moment by moment, we live in an unfolding space in which nothing is ever truly known. Given this reality, we do well to use the gift of prospection, that is, the ability to see many possible futures.

PROSPECTION

As discussed, our minds tend to spend a great deal of time in either the past or the future. More often than not, our future planning system (prospection) goes awry as we spend too much energy concerned with the future, resulting in anxiety and depression. In an article titled "Depression and Prospection," Ann Marie Roepke and Martin Seligman discuss three types of faulty prospection:

1. Poor generation of possible futures. We don't generate many possible options for the future. This type of prospection often ends up in an either-or view of future possibilities.
2. Poor evaluation of possible futures. We evaluate what

can happen and generate several options, but they are all negative.

3. Negative belief about the future. We don't do any evaluation and don't come up with any options. We jump to "there's no hope."[3]

As mentioned earlier, the brain is a prediction machine. In relation to the unknown, the brain tends to predict a horrible future. When we imagine a horrible future, we can become depressed. However, if the brain is trained to pay attention, it can be conditioned to predict positive outcomes as well. This is where mindfulness is helpful and allows us to engage with a balanced perspective. It rewires the brain. It creates different connections.

Sometimes it's good to think about the future. We need to plan, use a calendar, set goals, and so on. However, in thinking about the future we tend to think we can control all the causes and conditions that make an outcome possible. Thinking this way brings a false sense of security and more anxiety. We cannot control all of the causes and conditions that make our lives function well. We cannot control the future.

PLEASURE IN THE UNKNOWN

Cognitively, we know life is transient, impermanent, and unreliable. Yet we still waste an inordinate amount of time fearing and fighting the unknown. In his book *The Wisdom of Insecurity*, Alan Watts says, "The meaning and purpose of dancing is the dance. Like music, also, it [life] is fulfilled in each moment of its course. You do not play a sonata in order to reach the final chord. And if the meaning of things were simply an end, composers would write nothing but finales."[4]

Finding pleasure in the unknown is the adventure that makes us human. It's enjoying the mystery that is life rather than trying to solve the mysteries of life.

LEARNING THAT INFORMS

We can let the present guide our future. On the path of life, we learn lessons. We can let this learning inform our lives going forward. If I make a business decision that doesn't turn out well, does that inform future decisions? If I act in an unskillful way or say something inappropriate that causes harm to another, do I learn to make a different choice next time? The point isn't to beat myself up over mistakes. We're going to make them. That's part of being human. The point is to let what I learned from my mistakes inform my life right now, as well as in the future.

I was coaching a team and one participant said, "This last couple of weeks have been really hard. I haven't talked to one of my brothers in nine years, and I just found out he has stage four cancer. I'm realizing how petty our conflict was, and we both feel heartbroken that we haven't talked for so long."

I asked her what she felt was going to be most important about going through this situation right now.

"To see him," she said. "I'm going to try to get to California to see him in the next couple of weeks."

Then I asked how this experience is going to inform her life going forward.

"Don't hold a grudge."

In that moment, she learned an important lesson about what it is to hold on to hurt and carry a grudge. Her action of not speaking to her brother may or may not have been the right decision in the moments when they weren't speaking. There was no way to know. The point wasn't to pass judgment but for her to consider what she learned and how that can inform her present and future. Maybe not speaking to him was exactly what needed to happen because she learned a valuable lesson. Once again, the situation is both-and, not either-or.

The key idea is not getting caught up in the past, beating yourself up, ruminating, and so on. Let the past inform the present and the future so that you can act more skillfully.

To learn from our experience, we need to be able to consider the experience and simultaneously question it. For example, the woman who didn't speak to her brother could acknowledge her decision and also ask herself if it was the right one. She can be curious about what happened and what she can learn from it for the future at the same time she embraces the facts as they are.

Curiosity is an important trait, especially as it pertains to the future. The best way to kill curiosity is to believe we know. If we know we're right, that things will never change, that the future will be a certain way, then there's no reason to wonder about possible outcomes. We already "know" them. To practice a new skill like meditation, we must be curious about the possible future outcome. We must believe tomorrow could be different. Why would we read a book like this and attempt the skills discussed if we didn't think doing so could positively affect our future?

At the same time, however, it's naïve to believe everything we hear and read. We always want to check in with our own experience for validation. In her book *Faith: Trusting Your Own Deepest Experience*, Sharon Salzberg encourages us to be in touch with what the Buddhist tradition describes as "bright faith."[5] *Bright faith* believes something could be helpful to us (like this book or meditation or switching jobs) but continually checks with our experience to make sure it is indeed helping. In pursuit of a better future, bright faith keeps us in touch with our ability to discern and discriminate, and it allows our natural curiosity to question and experiment. *Blind faith*, on the other hand, looks to an external source for validation. Even when we are suffering, when our experience tells us something is not working, blind faith presses forward because that's what society or religion or our boss says we should do. Blind faith isn't questioning or curious. It causes us to override our own hearts and minds and blindly push forward based on external sources.

Salzberg also encourages us to admit fear about the future and, at the same time, let go of our need to feel in control at all times. For leaders, this is perhaps the most important twofold skill to learn: not denying fear of the unknown future while letting go of the need to control it. Denying fear about the future can result in blind optimism, or refusing to admit that things are not going well. This can cause leaders to ignore advice, make unwise decisions, and more. Trying to control the uncontrollable future often results in greed and fraud, as we've seen. If we don't acknowledge our fear, it will keep us running around on the dot, striving to take control. As a result, we lose touch with our heart, mind, and true experience. We remain stuck in our old patterns and unwise actions.

Salzberg encourages us to see how the rigid past and our limited scope of the future keep us from connecting to all of the possibilities only found in the present moment and in trust.

A TRANSACTIONAL LOOK AT THE UNKNOWN

A big part of a leader's transactional life involves decision-making: thinking through decisions, communicating those decisions, working with the team to carry out the decisions, and so on. Leaders have access to decision rights that individual contributors don't, such as who gets hired and fired, who gets promoted and who doesn't, and how the organization uses its time and money. At some level, all of these decisions involve the unknown. How we relate to that unknowing space affects the quality of those decisions, which in turn affects the well-being of those we lead. Thus, it's important to learn how to transact from trust rather than fear when we relate to the unknown.

TRANSACTING FROM FEAR

This book has showcased examples of suffering I've witnessed in my consulting business. In each case, the unwise actions that led to suffering were taken from a place of fear—fear of not getting what the person thought he should get or trying to avoid what the person didn't want. Anytime we are stuck in fear, our actions will result in suffering. It can't be any other way.

For example, if I feel overwhelmed and don't see how I'm going to accomplish everything on my list, I'm stuck in fear of the unknown. Of necessity, this fear will result in unskillful actions that cause suffering. I might snap at my partner for not taking out the trash. She will probably be hurt, and she might snap back. More suffering. If I'm worried that my performance at work is suffering and I'm compulsively replaying a potential review with my boss, I'm stuck in fear of the unknown. I might decide Friday that my team has to work Saturday to finish something I should have done weeks ago. My team suffers. Transacting from a place of fear can only lead to suffering for all involved.

TRANSACTING FROM TRUST

Effective leaders need to know how to plan and organize, both of which involve looking toward the future, the great unknown. The key is doing so with an open hand, knowing we are not in control of all the causes and conditions that may or may not create the outcomes we would prefer.

Planning

In business, if we want to bring a new product to market

or create a new piece of software, we need to plan and take action to execute the plan. Sometimes as leaders, we get attached to the thought that we will make this happen. We dismiss the fact that it takes many hands to bring such a plan to fruition. When we start planning for every possible contingency, we experience high levels of anxiety. We also run into the stark reality that we can't control all the causes and conditions, which leads many leaders into frustration and an inability to get a good night's sleep.

There is nothing wrong with planning and setting goals or the desire to create something amazing. The key is how we relate to the unknown elements in our planning, goal setting, and desiring. We typically relate to the unknown from fear, wanting to control every variable and predict every outcome. If you're paying attention, you'll quickly learn that you don't control anything.

Businesses spend so much time searching for *the* magic bullet that will allow them to systematize and control the future. The problem is, there is no magic bullet. There's no fool-proof planning system that will work every time. There's no magical leader who has discovered the secret sauce to success.

Since there's no magic bullet for controlling the future, we do well to approach planning with bright faith. We can set goals, plan ahead, and pursue the path that seems best, while continually checking in with our experience. We can hold our plans with an open hand, allowing the future to emerge as it will. Organizations want to control outcomes, yet the innovation needed for businesses' continued success requires a regular practice of letting go to allow ideas to emerge. How ironic.

As humans, we are all subject to the vicissitudes of life. In our planning we need to remember life is by nature transient and impermanent. We can't control all the conditions and causes. We can't control what people are going to say, what they're going to do, and how they're going to do it. We can, however, choose how to respond to not having that control. As I like to say, relax. Nothing is under control.

Pursuing goals takes action in the present. In fact, all we have is the present moment. It's worthwhile to take the actions that seem to give us the best possibility of having the best outcome, but we must recognize that we don't know what's going to happen in the future. We must hold goals with an open hand, while still taking the steps in the present to get there. When we hold the future with an open hand, we're free to respond and choose instead of react.

One pitfall to planning is that we zero in on one goal and lose sight of the many hopes we have for our lives, personally and professionally. In business, we might focus solely on making as much money as possible or bringing a single product to market. It's not that we shouldn't plan for and pursue these things; businesses do need to make money, after all. However, we set ourselves up for disappointment if we zero in on one outcome and that outcome doesn't come to fruition.

When we zero in on one plan, we don't desire enough for ourselves. As Walt Whitman once said, we are multitudes. We have more than one hope or goal. Our additional hopes and dreams get lost in our often fear-driven pursuit of that one thing. When we plan from a place of trust and openness, however, we can keep our eye on more than just one hope. We can plan for the business's financial gain *and* how that gain might be used to help the employees or the community. We can plan for bringing a new product to market *and* how that product might help users be more productive in their own lives. Planning from a place of trust allows us to look at the bigger picture because we're not caught up in the ambition and striving that pull us away from acting on our better nature. We can actually be curious about who we might become on our path to achieving the goal, regardless of whether we achieve it.

Dr. Chris Feudtner, a palliative pediatric oncologist, worked with parents who were undergoing likely one of life's greatest losses, the loss of a child.[6] Clearly, these parents held as their greatest hope a cure for their child. Yet, as Dr. Feudtner shared the horrific news that their child might not be cured, he discovered these parents had other hopes: that their child be in no pain and that the child be able to return home for their last few days. He found that hope doesn't entail one solidified notion of the future. Likewise, as we shift our understanding of hope and embrace the idea of bright faith over blind faith, we find a more meaningful way to plan for future, unknown moments in our lives and businesses.

With this mindset toward planning and hope, how we measure success expands and takes on a broader depth. Dr. Clayton Christensen, Harvard Business School professor and author, asks us to consider these three questions toward constructing a better future for ourselves:

1. "How will I be sure that I will be successful and happy in my career?
2. How will I be sure that my relationships with my spouse, my children, and my extended family and close friends become an enduring source of happiness?
3. How will I live a life of integrity and stay out of jail?"[7]

After graduation, two of Dr. Christensen's Rhodes Scholar classmates went to jail, and many others created lives that became riddled with difficult relationships and less-than-satisfactory careers. In his book *How Will You Measure Your Life*, Dr. Christensen earnestly posits that it isn't about having the *right* answers to life's problems. Instead, it's about considering what will provide the best life for ourselves and others in the face of life's problems. Discovering what this is takes paying attention, practicing bright faith, and seeing the many hopes you have for your life.

Goal Setting

If I set a goal and I'm relating to that goal from a belief in a fixed self, I become attached to the goal. In other words, I become the goal. If I don't achieve the goal, it says something about me. I will slip into judging myself or my team for not achieving the goal, and suffering results. If I do achieve the goal, that says something about me as well: I'm awesome. Now I'm going to do everything in my power to maintain my awesomeness. When something happens that causes me to realize I'm not so awesome, I'm going to suffer. The reality is, meeting or not meeting the goal is just part of the human experience. It's not a permanent thing or a comment on my inherent value. The more we believe that achieving a goal means something about us, the more we suffer on our path to achieve it.

Have you ever been falling asleep, then you wake up

and try to get back to sleep? Your big goal is to fall asleep, and what happens? You don't fall asleep. You become so attached to the idea that achieving this particular goal will mean something for you (maybe that you aren't so crabby and tired the next day) that just the thought of not sleeping is enough to keep you awake all night. Then you become frustrated and agitated because you can't fall asleep—you can't reach the goal.

Also, in the process, you lose sight of the good things you do have; for example, you're lying in a warm, cozy bed, and in the morning, you get to do work you love. It becomes a vicious cycle. You get increasingly frustrated and become less effective at falling asleep. Plus, when you are attached, you get sucked into the illusion that achieving the goal will be the sole reason for your happiness.

Pitfalls

Becoming attached to a goal as just described is one pitfall to goal setting. Here are five more:

1. Being so focused on the future that we miss the actions we need to take right now. When we set goals, we're looking toward something in the future that hasn't happened yet. Our actions, however, can only take place in the present. We can't get so caught up in

the goal out there in the future that we're not present to what actions need to be taken now, both in terms of achieving the goal and other areas of life. When we develop this narrow future focus, the road ahead becomes hazy and we miss the steps we can take right now (figure 9.1).

2. Being so focused on the future that we miss what we already have. In goal setting, we're naturally focused on what's missing—the thing we're trying to achieve. As a result, we can miss what's present; that is, what we've already received in the process of working toward the goal, who we're becoming, and what we can be grateful for right now.

3. Creating anxiety for ourselves because we haven't achieved the goal. If we're focused solely on what we don't have in the future, we become increasingly anxious about getting there.

4. Believing it's a comment on us personally if we don't achieve the goal. In our individualistic culture rife with ambition, achievement, and snobbery, we have bought into the idea that we can and should make anything happen. We've lost sight of the fact that thousands of causes and conditions intervene between the making and achieving (or not) of a goal. The truth is, stuff happens. Sometimes we fall on bad luck. Sometimes we don't have the wind at our back. Not achieving a goal is not a referendum on who we are as people. Philosopher Alain de Botton described

snobbery as the phenomenon of taking a small part of who someone is and using it to come to a complete vision of that person.[8] If someone loses his house, we view him as a loser—not someone who happened to lose his home. We make the loss personal and blame the person's inability to manage money, when that might not be the case.

5.   Believing there's something in the future that will make us happy. First, you can't be happy in the future because the future doesn't exist as an ultimate reality. It is a conventional one. Of course, this doesn't mean that we don't set goals and that we don't live a life of integrity with care. That would be like denying I have a body when I stub my toe. Second, we're just not that good at predicting what will make us happy in the future. When we imagine the future, we make a lot of errors. We leave things out (e.g., we want to write a book and forget that we have a day job and a family), we confuse our current feelings with our future ones (e.g., we think the money we spend now on new Chuck Taylors will make us feel good tomorrow), and we adapt to realities that aren't so good to begin with (i.e., when the difficult times arise, we convince ourselves that things aren't that bad).[9] Of all of the pitfalls, this is likely the one that leaves most leaders stymied by their lack of fulfillment once the goal is achieved.

Figure 9.1. The hazy road also represents what we have right now and don't see or appreciate because we're so focused on the future goal.

The way we live in the present is what matters most to attaining any goal. We can only achieve our goals with our present actions because that's all we have. When we let go of the idea that happiness depends on achieving our goals, we can relax and appreciate what we have now. We can set goals, pursue them, and do everything we can to achieve them, knowing it's okay if we don't attain them. Achieving goals or not achieving goals is just part of the ebb and flow of life.

SMARTO Goals

When we set goals, they should be SMARTO goals: **S**pecific, **M**easurable, **A**ttainable, **R**ealistic, and **T**imebound.[10] The O stands for planning for **O**bstructions.

- **S**pecific. Your stated goal should state exactly what you want to accomplish. For example, "We will achieve 10 percent growth in sales by June 2021" is specific. "We will grow the business" is not.
- **M**easurable. You should be able to measure whether you've reached your goal. Again, by having a specific percentage or number, you will know whether you've met the goal.
- **A**ttainable (or achievable). The goal should be something that can be done. We might want to grow the business by 50 percent in one year, but we have to ask ourselves if that's truly attainable.
- **R**ealistic. The goal should be something that makes sense given resources, market conditions, and so on. For example, 10 percent growth by the end of the year might be attainable but not realistic given the current market conditions.
- **T**ime-bound. The goal has a specified end date.
- **O**bstructions. Plan for obstructions you might encounter in the process of achieving your goal. For example, if you're trying to grow a business, you want to think through potential obstructions to that growth, like having people resign. Thinking through future possibilities is not a problem unless you get stuck in fear.[11]

Setting SMARTO goals is worth your team's time. You will benefit from having a specific vision of what you are trying to accomplish. You can talk through the fact that you're going from point A to point B, the path you'll follow to get there, the key performance indicators, and problems you might face along the way. Just remember to keep an open hand and beware of the pitfalls.

There are many uncontrollable variables in the space we call the unknown. When we find ourselves spending too much time and energy trying to predict the future and as a result, are not enjoying our lives, the answer is simple: come back to the present. We will never figure out all the mysteries of this life. Rather than try, it's better to become a skilled surfer, riding the ever-changing waves of life as they roll our way.

In *The Teachings of Don Juan*, Don Juan advises Carlos Castaneda to:

> ...look at every path closely and deliberately. Try it as many times as you think necessary. Then ask yourself alone one question...does this path have a heart? If it does, the path is good; if it doesn't it is of no use. Both paths lead nowhere, but one has a heart, the other doesn't. One makes for a joyful journey, as long as you follow it, you are one with it. The other will make you curse your life. One makes you strong; the other weakens you.[12]

We do well to take this advice to heart. What path brings

you the most joy and meaning? What path contributes to your ability to thrive and to help others do the same? Remember, we're all connected in navigating the mystery of the unknown. Together, we wake up to all that is possible and true.

EXERCISE: MEDITATION ON DEATH

Lesson: If you want a certainty to cling to, there is only one in life: the body will stop breathing. This is the one true known. Yet, even in that certainty, there is uncertainty because we don't know when death will happen or how the body will stop breathing.

Goal: This meditation can assist us in becoming more comfortable with the reality of the unknown and uncertainty alongside certainty. By listening to the answers that arise in this meditation, we can find our own true path in the moment.

Setup: Find a quiet space in which you can steady the attention. Sit in a comfortable position, relaxed and alert.

Process: Begin by gently placing your attention on the breath. Allow the attention to become collected and still. Allow the tension to settle. Focus gently on the breath.

Once the attention is steadied and gently resting, allow yourself to consider the reality that death is certain. The body will stop breathing. Meditate on that reality for a few minutes.

Next, consider the uncertainty of death's timing. The certainty is that death will occur. The uncertainty is when. Allow your mind to reflect on this reality for a few moments.

Then reflect on the following. Given death's certainty and the timing's uncertainty, consider these questions: "What should I do? How will this certainty/uncertainty inform my action going forward?"

You may sit in quiet meditation on these questions as long as you like. The intention is not to come up with answers but instead to simply see what arises. At times, you may notice clear thoughts coming to you. Other times, it may seem like not much is occurring at all. Simply sit and meditate.

When you finish this meditation, you can journal about the thoughts that arose.

This meditation can become part of your daily mindfulness practice, a mantra of sorts: "Death is certain. Timing is uncertain. Given that, now what should I do?"[13]

PART III

LEADERSHIP DEVELOPMENT CULTURE

Leaders have an incalculable influence on an organization's culture. They have access to key decision rights not available to an individual contributor. Leaders decide who gets hired and fired, which projects are funded, and how their team spends its time. In other words, they make decisions about the organization's use of its most valuable resources: people, time, and money.

Because leaders have this incalculable influence on the current and future path of an organization, it's worth our time to develop them. Leaders are not born with the transformational and transactional skills to lead; they need to be developed in the five relationships we've been discussing.

That said, leaders alone are not responsible for the organization's culture. Leaders need to be awake and paying attention themselves, but everyone in an organization influences the organization's culture and makes decisions about the kind of culture they want to work in. Every time someone chooses not to gossip about a coworker and goes directly to the individual, every time someone takes responsibility for a decision rather than blaming someone else, people are making decisions about the culture. Everyone in an organization is responsible for those decisions, not just the leadership team.

When we develop leaders, we take the first step toward

developing the larger culture everyone participates in. Chapter 10 discusses the idea of why we must develop leaders, and chapter 11 outlines how to make a leadership development plan work for long-term, sustainable results.

CHAPTER 10

WHY WE MUST DEVELOP LEADERS

"Just because you are CEO, don't think you have landed. You must continually increase your learning, the way you think, and the way you approach the organization."

—INDRA NOOYI, CEO, PEPSICO

Timmy was an excellent walker. I mean, no one walked better than Timmy. He walked to class, he walked onto the football field, he walked home from school. Sometimes Timmy even ran, and he was good at that too.

One day, Timmy's dad saw him walking with his friends after school and thought, "Man, that kid can walk!" When Timmy got home, his dad sat him down and said, "Timmy, I saw you walking today. You walk really, really well, son. Tomorrow, I'm going to let you drive to school.

You're so good at walking, I just know you'll be an excellent driver."

Ridiculous, right? But that's what we do with leaders all the time. We think that because they're excellent at the job we hired them to do, they're going to be excellent leaders and managers, so we move them into a new position and give them no training or instruction on how to actually lead. The average leader is in a leadership role for about a decade before she receives any form of leadership training or development. One day the person is selling widgets, the next day she is sitting in a meeting with four salespeople looking at her for direction, and the person has never led a team in her life.

This chapter discusses the need to create formal leadership development structures within our organizations.

LEADERS WITHOUT SKILLS

When we don't take the time to develop leaders, suffering occurs on several levels. Without the key transformational skills discussed in this book, leaders get stuck in the reactivity of fear. They potentially experience anxiety, stress, and depression. As seen in my story and others', leaders develop poor coping behaviors, neglect friends and family, and experience significantly decreased well-being.

Because organizations are made up of people, the personal anxieties overflow into the workplace. Organizations run on fear and adrenaline. Leaders can't think clearly because they're stressed out. As a result, they make horrible decisions that end up costing the company time, money, and energy. They may even land the organization in lawsuits because of these poor decisions.

Leadership development is an investment. At minimum, it's an investment to minimize risk: risk of losing employees, risk of retribution, risk of creating a burned-out toxic culture. At maximum, it's an investment to create an organization of people who have a higher level of well-being and who enjoy working in their chosen place of employment.

TOXIC CULTURES

Toxic leadership (leaders who are not supportive of those who work for them and do not align what they do with what they say) can lead to extreme results. An organization that has toxic leadership will have a toxic culture. It can't be any other way.

We often have a particular image of what a toxic manager looks like. We have visions of the schoolyard bully, aggressive and loud-mouthed with an ax to grind with anyone who crosses her path. This is the manager we often want to avoid and that much of the literature highlights as the person not to be.

While this may be true in some instances, it isn't always the case. In an article for *The New York Times*, Jon Picoult examined several instances where leadership didn't fit the stereotypical toxic image, yet the effect on the culture was just as devastating. One case involved the Wells Fargo scandal in which 5,300 lower level employees created fake accounts to meet sales quotas set forth by management. All 5,300 employees were fired. Another case involved Volkswagen engineers who attempted to work around the United States' emissions requirements by outfitting cars with software that would provide misleading information to pass emissions tests. In both instances, managers were fully aware of what was occurring. They established the goals that drove the behavior and then rewarded employees when they achieved those goals, not caring about how they were achieved. These managers weren't described as the yelling, bullyish types we often think of as creating environments in which people would lie and steal to be successful. Nonetheless, they created environments that clearly told employees what was most important: winning and getting results at all costs, including lying, cheating, and violating everyone's ultimate best interests.[1]

When leaders function on fear and adrenaline, they

create unsustainable behaviors within themselves and others. These managers aren't necessarily nefarious characters, but their negative influence on those who report to them is still unmistakable. Due to leaders' fear, employees come to work stressed-out and disengaged. At best, they stop taking care of themselves and achieve solid bottom-line results at high costs to personal well-being. At worst, they violate laws and their own human decency.

Unsustainable behavior results from not paying attention and making unwise choices. Lost in the world of ambition, status, and fear, leaders spin their wheels, lose money on projects, and don't communicate well with their team or other departments. As a result, products aren't released on time, salespeople don't meet their quotas, and clients are left unhappy. Leaders then react in even greater fear.

Toxicity in a work culture shows up in other ways as well. Leaders try to "save" time by multitasking in meetings. They show up late, ignore the presenter, and work on their phones or laptops. Meetings run late because the group was waiting for the stragglers, and leaders rush off to their next thing stressed-out because they're late. All of this toxicity trickles down to the individual contributors, who learn the expected behavior by watching—not only listening to—those in leadership.

I've worked with a company for a few years, and the

leaders are fairly awake to the transformational truths discussed in this book. Still, one of their CEOs recently sent an email to me and another coach saying, "I've received some feedback from the team. They said the team coaching process isn't really effective."

There are eight teams within this company, and over the previous three months this CEO's teams had been consistently showing up without getting their actions done. Their excuse each time was that they're busy, they've got a lot going on, and so on.

Shortly after I received the CEO's email, I had a call with the COO and her group. She was stressed-out. She complained about how much she had going on. Based on the email and the phone conversation, I knew exactly why the rest of the team was showing up the way they were. They were following the example of the leaders.

The actions of these leaders impacted everyone around them. When I met with the whole executive team, they all started chiming out of the same songbook: "We're all so busy, we're all so busy." They weren't taking responsibility for their actions or the way in which they were relating. They weren't seeing how they were creating the experience they were having. They blamed each other, the lack of time, workload, poor quarterly returns—anything other than themselves. With compassion, it only took a gentle reminder to bring them to awareness of how they were relating and to the stories they were all telling themselves.

If leaders are not being trained in the transformational and transactional leadership skills, they easily fall into the trap of relating from fear. They focus on the latest and greatest—the urgent, not the important. They are on the treadmill, running as fast as they can and getting nowhere. They never feel like they have enough time. They're never certain how to make enough money for the business. They're not taking care of themselves or spending time with family and friends. They're trying to control things they can't control, working twelve hours a day or more to get everything done because they believe they have to do it all. They are relating to time, money, their identity, people, and the unknown from a place of fear.

In their investigation of risk culture in banking, authors Nicola Bianchi and Franco Fiordelisi found the "tone from the top" had the greatest influence on the culture when it came to unnecessary risk. The other three variables considered were accountability, effective communication, and incentives.[2]

No one knows how to magically lead a group of people or how to work with the vicissitudes of life that can and will find us. Remember Timmy? He knew how to walk, but that doesn't mean he knows how to drive. Skills have to be taught and awareness cultivated within the organizational context, and this must be seen as vital to creating a thriving business with thriving people.

Leading with finely tuned transformational and transactional skills helps entire organizations navigate the unpredictable world in which we all live. These skills also increase the likelihood of achieving exceptional business results. However, it doesn't guarantee them. Furthermore, implementing leadership development and mindfulness in an organization for the sole purpose of increasing the company's bottom line doesn't work. As soon as you put money front and center and attempt to align all actions around this one narrow scope, all other great behaviors (kindness, generosity, teamwork, etc.) begin to erode. People don't like feeling manipulated and aren't likely to put forth extra effort to employ the practices, especially if the tone from the top is to make more money.

There are many examples in which positive emotion and positive work environments contribute to excellent bottom-line results and help individuals thrive, even when the tough times hit.[3] Incorporating a program to cultivate mindfulness, compassion, wisdom, and essential transactional leadership skills requires effort. If leaders and their organizations are interested in more than only meeting the demands of the bottom line, both for themselves and the people they lead, then the effort will be worth it.

The next chapter discusses how to implement a development program that works.

CHAPTER 11

HOW TO MAKE LEADERSHIP DEVELOPMENT WORK

"Our emerging workforce is not interested in command-and-control leadership. They don't want to do things because I said so; they want to do things because they want to do them."

—IRENE ROSENFELD, CEO, MONDELĒZ INTERNATIONAL

Company Y decided to have a one-day leadership development seminar. The CEO brought all of the employees into the conference room on a Wednesday morning. They brought in a consultant, who talked for three hours, handed out some worksheets, and left. The employees went to lunch or back to their desks and never talked about the information again. No one reinforced the concepts, no one told the employees, "This is the way we're doing things now." It was a one-day rah-rah session in the flavor of the month.

Company Z hired a consultant to systematically take its leaders through a leadership training pathway. Training consisted of a series of sessions that occurred over the course of a full year. Leaders met once a month to watch a training video and participate in live group sessions to discuss the concepts and applications. Outside the training room, everyone in the company reinforced the ideas presented and practiced what was learned in the training sessions. The organizational leaders also created documents with their newfound approaches and gave them to all newly hired managers.

Which company is more likely to make leadership development work? There's nothing wrong with a one-day seminar, but it's not a leadership development plan. This chapter provides three key factors for creating a culture of leadership development throughout the organization.

TAKE RESPONSIBILITY

For any leadership development platform to work, the top-level executives have to own it, value it, and make it the way of doing things in their organization. As noted earlier, the tone from the top matters greatly. No matter what consulting group or platform is used, executives have to make the program their own. One of the biggest mistakes companies make is half-heartedly implementing a development program that starts to look like someone else's material. Without full integration—including company branding and logos on the handouts—the concepts and practices sit "out there" and employees don't get the sense that they are their own.

For example, my Waking Up a Leader online program is all on video. I give the training, but all the branding gets owned by the company. They put their logo on the materials and deploy the program fully in their energy. I explain that I'm the person who is going to walk them through the training, but none of my branding is present. It is also a full partnership. The company recruits people in the organization who will teach the program to upcoming leaders and eventually creates a full-blown culture based on the concepts described in this book, in their own voice and in their own context.

For leadership development to work, *every* leader in the organization has to own it. Through word and deed, they all have to communicate that it's necessary, important, and the way they do things.

COMMIT THE TIME AND RESOURCES

Part of owning the development is setting aside the time and resources to put it in place. Leadership development doesn't happen in optional seminars on Saturday and Sunday. It requires a formal training and development structure. Setting aside this time sends the signal of importance in the organization. The old saying "Put your money where your mouth is" applies here.

Nothing is more telling than hearing how a company wants to move its culture toward leadership development, yet they've designated no budget for the process. If you want great leaders and a great culture, the line item on your budget needs to reflect this goal, just like the other many things that are budgeted for every year. If you don't budget for training, you really don't want it.

Your company may not have a lot of extra expendable cash. Then do something with the resources you do have. Don't put training last on your list. Company-wide leadership development should be seen as a necessity, not a nicety.

You don't have the time not to develop your leaders. The cost of not making time could be a lawsuit. "We're too busy" is not a reason to forgo formal training. In fact, that thinking is why you need transformational training, to wake up leaders to a new way of relating to time as well as money, the self, friendships, and the unknown.

ESTABLISH A FORMAL STRUCTURE

A few years ago, I asked one executive how her company was training its leaders. She said, "Oh, it happens informally."

"Really?" I replied. "How does that happen?"

"Some leaders meet with their team, and some leaders meet with other leaders in peer groups."

"So, there are peer groups that specifically meet?"

"Well, no, they just, you know, meet when they have to work on projects together."

Basically, she was saying that the informal leadership development plan consisted of people showing up at meetings from time to time.

Imagine Timmy learning to drive "informally." How's that going to work? It's not. Learning any new skill takes conscious, deliberate training and practice. Implementing an organization-wide leadership development program is no different. It requires an intentional, reproducible, and sustainable model for developing leaders and cultivating them throughout their life cycle in the company.

The formal structure itself will vary from company to

company based on resources. It might be a weekly discussion of a leadership book with specific actions derived from the learning and practices instilled or monthly training with a consultant. The key is to make it intentional and to structure it so employees can apply it. Training should not stay in the theoretical. Employees need to understand how to apply what they learn in specific situations and be given specific practices and actions.

As pointed out earlier, companies can make a lot of money without implementing a formal leadership development training structure. But don't be deluded. People want more out of their job than making money. If you want to be competitive in today's market, your yardstick of success has to be much bigger than offering employees a paycheck.

Employees today want to get their work done *and* have a good level of well-being. They want to feel proud of the company they work for. They want to know the company cares about its employees. Caring does not mean they have the best bonus structures. Caring means the company supports its employees in their development and growth as long as they're with the company. Caring means employees have opportunities for being creative and innovative. If your company doesn't offer these things, people will eventually look for them elsewhere.

Think about individuals in your company who already

have leadership qualities. These individuals still need the structure and guidance to develop those skills. Without an intentional plan to cultivate and develop leaders, your business will not grow, at least not to the extent it could. Its growth will be haphazard. In addition, your company will experience HR problems, such as managers who don't know how to speak to employees and say awkward things like, "Oh my gosh, you're pregnant again?"

As we've discussed throughout the book, leadership training should take place on two planes: transformational and transactional. Leaders need to be mindful of what is actually happening in the workplace. They need to be able to distinguish fact from story in interactions with coworkers. Effective leaders practice mindfulness in their own lives. They pay attention to their thoughts and emotions, and they know how to bring their focus back to the present facts when it strays to the past or future.

Effective leaders also know how to skillfully transact with external phenomena, be it time, money, people, the unknown, or their own identity. They know how to set goals and pursue them with an open hand, remaining present even as they look to the future. They understand the company's policies and procedures; they know how to delegate, organize their calendar, and use their time efficiently and effectively to tackle tasks and projects.

If you're struggling in your leadership role, it might be because you're like Timmy. Someone saw your skill in what you were hired to do and fast-tracked you to a leadership role without giving you formal training. Take responsibility for your own development, even if your company hasn't implemented a formal plan.

If you're the person in your company who has decision rights regarding leadership development, take action to see that your team is at least getting some formal and structured training. Remember, leadership development training isn't a one-time rah-rah meeting. It's something that needs to be formally implemented company-wide.

CONCLUSION

When people read leadership books and listen to leadership podcasts, they often do so for one of two reasons: either they have a toxic team and they're trying to figure out what to do, or their buddy has a toxic team and they don't want to be that guy or gal. They don't want to be the bad manager or bad leader in a bad organization. They either have the problem presently or they're trying to prevent it from happening in the first place.

My goal is to help both readers.

No matter where you are on the leadership spectrum, you can wake up to a new way of leading. Mindfulness is not reserved for the chosen few. It's a skill you can learn and practice daily. Doing so will transform the way you relate to your thoughts, emotions, coworkers, and the vicissitudes of life. When you stay present, you can see what's happening, talk to yourself about how you're relating, and bring yourself back to the facts. You have the power to choose how you respond. You can manage your relationships with time, money, the self, friendships, and the unknown from a place of trust. As a result, you will lead more effectively and with less suffering for yourself and others.

NOW WHAT?

Here are three suggestions for putting these transformational and transactional skills to work.

1. START MEDITATING

To learn to pay attention and shift the way you relate to the external world, you need to develop a daily meditation practice. Even if it's only ten minutes a day, meditating is the key to making this internal transformational shift.

If you don't know where to start, check out my website at www.wakingupaleader.com. There you'll find tons of guided meditations, some related to the five relationships we've discussed.

2. PICK ONE OF THE FIVE RELATIONSHIPS TO WORK ON FIRST

You're probably aware of places where you are not effectively managing your relationships with time, money, your identity, friendships, and the unknown. Working on these relationships is a process. Rather than try to change everything all at once, which isn't possible anyway, pick one of the five to start with.

For me, the first relationship I needed to manage better was time. My first step was to be more specific about what I was saying yes to at work. This required an internal, transformational shift in the way I saw my identity. I had to stop saying yes in an effort to get approval and maintain my sense of self. I only said yes to things when I knew I was absolutely the one who had to do them.

Next, I started letting go of the idea that I didn't have enough time. I had been conditioned to believe this. Anytime I realized that I was complaining about a lack of time, I literally told myself, "Nope! You're just telling yourself that. You have all the time you need to do the things you need to get done."

Recently, a friend gave me some positive feedback regarding how I've changed in this area. He's known me for over a decade, so he knew the miserable, stressed Daphne described in the introduction. He said, "Your ease around time and the way you move through the world—you're so different now than when I met you ten years ago."

The reason I was so different is that my relationship to time had changed.

The same can be true for you. Pick the relationship where you consistently relate from fear. Imagine what it will be like in ninety days or six months when the relationship is thriving. A good standard of thriving is the amount of peace, calm, and joy you have, regardless of what's happening around you. Also, you'll notice you're not complaining as much about that relationship—how little time or money you have, for example.

3. TALK WITH YOUR TEAM

When you're awakened as a leader, you have the opportunity to support your team as they wake up to this new mindset and way of relating. Facilitate a conversation about the five relationships with your team. Consider where you are as a team in terms of managing each one. If you need help figuring out how to start this discussion, go to www.wakingupaleader.com. There you'll find handouts and an outline for a team workshop.

Most of all, remember to relax. Nothing is under control.

ACKNOWLEDGMENTS

Many people made this book possible and were the supportive "giants" on whose shoulders I've had the privilege and blessing to stand.

Many wise guides have walked the earth long before me, guides who have allowed us all to look deeper within our own hearts and minds to see the truth. To all of those brave hearts, I am forever indebted.

To the many brave leaders who know there is a way to live a fulfilling life and have work that is meaningful in the world, how I have been blessed to sit with you, talk with you, laugh with you, and learn from you. You have challenged the assumptions of the way business should be done and take the exquisite risk to create environments that are as concerned with thriving as they are with generating a profit. You know who you are. Dr.

Larry Benz, your influence on me in that spirit cannot be overstated.

To Napier McCleary, the first person to tell me that seeing the world in this way changed his life after I presented the concepts to him. In that moment, I woke up to the possibility that this structure may be of benefit to many others. Thank you, Napier.

I am deeply grateful to two of my greatest teachers, Diana Chapman and Jim Dethmer, founders of the Conscious Leadership group and also my dearest friends. Words can almost not express my love for all that you've offered me in the spirit of growth, laughter, and love.

As this book came into being, I also benefited greatly from the advice, support, and writing prowess of Gail Fay and the entire team at Scribe Media. They are a fearless group of readers, writers, editors, designers, and accountability partners as well as an endless source of guidance and encouragement.

I am grateful to the thousands of scientists, researchers, psychologists, spiritual teachers, and wisdom seekers who have stood for the awakening in us all.

I am also deeply blessed to have learned directly from Dr. Martin Seligman and all of the other amazing instructors and professors in the Master of Applied Positive Psychology program at the University of Pennsylvania. My time in the program and the learnings I continue to gain as a member of the MAPP community cannot be overstated.

I would also like to share my words of appreciation with three of my beloved mindfulness teachers: Tara Brach, Jack Kornfield, and Sharon Salzberg. Each of them has inspired me in the direction of greater awakening in my personal and professional life, and I am honored to be one of their thousands of students.

I owe my deepest gratitude to my family and friends for their encouragement and cheerleading as well as listening and offering insights. These were some of the best moments in this writing process. Your wisdom, love, and kindness are the stuff of life that nurtured this book into being.

My unwavering appreciation to Marta, who, more times than not, was the one who listened as I rambled on about my ideas, read the very clunky first draft, kept my schedule from imploding, and simply helped me see the humor throughout the whole process.

My love and thanks to my mom, Sandra; my stepdad, Dennis; my brothers, Ben and Sheldon; and my two sisters-in-law, Lesley and Whitney. Your love is what brings me joy and makes the tough times much less tough.

And of course, thank you to my wife, Bridgit, and Gerty, our pup, for being there and always reminding me to remember to remember. Without your patience, support, encouragement, and love, this book would have remained just another good idea.

ABOUT THE
AUTHOR

DR. DAPHNE SCOTT is the founder of DS Leadership Life and the chief culture officer for Confluent Health. She is an expert at waking up leaders to a mindful way of leading, and given her improv comedy training, she brings a unique sense of humor to her work helping merged companies integrate cultures. Daphne holds a master's of applied positive psychology and is also a certified mindfulness meditation teacher. She hosts *The Super Fantastic Leadership Show* podcast and the series *Leadership in the Driver's Seat* on her YouTube channel. Learn more and read her blog at www.daphne-scott.com.

NOTES

PART I

1 Karl W. Kuhnert and Philip Lewis, "Transactional and Transformational Leadership: A Constructive/Developmental Analysis," *Academy of Management Review* 12, no. 4 (October 1987): 648.

2 Kuhnert and Lewis, 648.

CHAPTER 1

1 Matthias Siemer, Iris Mauss, and James J. Gross, "Same Situation—Different Emotions: How Appraisals Shape Our Emotions," *Emotion* 7, no. 3 (2007): 592.

2 Eric Anderson, Erika H. Siegel, and Lisa Feldman Barrett, "What You Feel Influences What You See: The Role of Affective Feelings in Resolving Binocular Rivalry," *Journal of Experimental Social Psychology* 47, no. 4 (July 2011): 856-860; Dalai Lama, *The Meaning of Life: Buddhist Perspectives on Cause and Effect* (New York: Simon and Schuster, 2005), 1-20.

3 Thomas Keating, *The Human Condition: Contemplation and Transformation* (Mahwah, NJ: Paulist Press, 1999), 14.

4 Adapted from William Hart, *The Art of Living: Vipassana Meditation as Taught by S. N. Goenka* (New York; Harper and Row, 1987), 132-146.

5 James O. Pawelski and D. J. Moores, eds., *The Eudaimonic Turn: Well-Being in Literary Studies* (Lanham, MD: Rowman & Littlefield, 2013), 1-2; James O. Pawelski, "Defining the 'Positive' in Positive Psychology: Part II. A Normative Analysis," *Journal of Positive Psychology* 11, no. 4 (July 3, 2016): 357-365.

6   Jack Kornfield, ed., *Teachings of the Buddha* (Boston, MA: Shambhala, 2012), 26–27.

7   David Whyte, *Consolations: The Solace, Nourishment, and Underlying Meaning of Everyday Words* (Langley, WA: Many Rivers Press, 2015), loc. 401, Kindle for Mac.

8   Martin E. P. Seligman, *Learned Optimism: How to Change Your Mind and Your Life* (New York: Vintage, 2006), 43–51.

9   Ethan Kross and Ozlem Ayduk, "Making Meaning out of Negative Experiences by Self-Distancing," *Current Directions in Psychological Science* 20, no. 3 (May 24, 2011): 187–191.

10   Bhikkhu Bodhi, *In the Buddha's Words: An Anthology of Discourses from the Pali Canon* (Somerville, MA; Wisdom Publications, 2005), 19.

CHAPTER 2

1   Jon Kabat-Zinn, *Wherever You Go, There You Are: Mindfulness Meditation in Everyday Life* (New York: Hachette Books, 2009), loc. 184, Kindle.

2   Keisuke Takano and Yoshihiko Tanno, "Self-Rumination, Self-Reflection, and Depression: Self-Rumination Counteracts the Adaptive Effect of Self-Reflection," *Behaviour Research and Therapy* 47, no. 3 (March 2009): 260–264; Sonja Lyubomirsky and Heidi S. Lepper, "A Measure of Subjective Happiness: Preliminary Reliability and Construct Validation," *Social Indicators Research* 46, no. 2 (February 1999): 137–155.

3   Richard J. Davidson, "Mindfulness-Based Cognitive Therapy and the Prevention of Depressive Relapse: Measures, Mechanisms, and Mediators," *JAMA Psychiatry* 73, no. 6 (April 2016): 547–548.

4   Daniel J. Siegel, *The Mindful Brain: Reflection and Attunement in the Cultivation of Well-Being* (New York: W.W. Norton & Company, 2007), 3–12; Daphne M. Davis and Jeffrey A. Hayes, "What Are the Benefits of Mindfulness? A Practice Review of Psychotherapy-Related Research," *Psychotherapy* 48, no. 2 (2011): 198; Yu-Qin Deng, Song Li, and Yi-Yuan Tang, "The Relationship between Wandering Mind, Depression, and Mindfulness," *Mindfulness* 5, no. 2 (April 2014): 124–128.

5   Paul Rozin and Edward B. Royzman, "Negativity Bias, Negativity Dominance, and Contagion," *Personality and Social Psychology Review* 5, no. 4 (November 1, 2001): 296–320.

6   Rick Hanson, *Hardwiring Happiness: The New Brain Science of Contentment, Calm, and Confidence* (New York: Harmony, 2016), 2.

7   Matthew A. Killingsworth and Daniel T. Gilbert, "A Wandering Mind Is an Unhappy Mind," *Science* 330, no. 6006 (November 12, 2010): 932.

8   Willoughby B. Britton, "Can Mindfulness Be Too Much of a Good Thing? The Value
    of a Middle Way," *Current Opinion in Psychology* 28 (August 2019): 159–165, https://doi.
    org/10.1016/j.copsyc.2018.12.011; Jared R. Lindahl, Nathan E. Fisher, David J. Cooper,
    Rochelle K. Rosen, and Willoughby B. Britton, "The Varieties of Contemplative Experience: A
    Mixed-Methods Study of Meditation-Related Challenges in Western Buddhists," *PloS One* 12,
    no. 5 (May 24, 2017): e0176239.

9   Britton, "Can Mindfulness Be Too Much of a Good Thing?" 159–165; Lindahl et al., "The
    Varieties of Contemplative Experience," 2–28.

CHAPTER 3

1   Brad Blanton, *Radical Honesty: How to Transform Your Life by Telling the Truth* (Stanley, VA:
    Sparrowhawk, 2005), 52.

2   Jack Kornfield, *The Wise Heart: A Guide to the Universal Teachings of Buddhist Psychology* (New
    York: Bantam Books, 2009), loc. 1612, Kindle for Mac.

3   Jon Kabat-Zinn, *Wherever You Go, There You Are: Mindfulness Meditation in Everyday Life* (New
    York: Hachette Books, 2009), loc. 184, Kindle.

4   Kabat-Zinn, loc. 1980, Kindle.

CHAPTER 4

1   Lisa Feldman Barrett, *How Emotions Are Made: The Secret Life of the Brain* (Boston: Houghton
    Mifflin, 2017), 145–146.

2   Barrett, 290; Lisa Feldman Barrett, "Solving the Emotion Paradox: Categorization and the
    Experience of Emotion," *Personality and Social Psychology Review* 10, no. 1 (2006): 20–46.

3   Blago Kirov, *Epictetus: Quotes and Facts* (Lulu Press,, 2016), loc. 225, Kindle for Mac.

4   William James, Frederick Burkhardt, Fredson Bowers, and Ignas K. Skrupskelis, *The Principles
    of Psychology*, vol. 1 (London: Macmillan, 1890), 402.

5   Albert Ellis, "The Revised ABC's of Rational-Emotive Therapy (RET)," *Journal of Rational-
    Emotive and Cognitive-Behavior Therapy* 9, no. 3 (Fall 1991): 139–172.

6   Barrett, *How Emotions Are Made*, 58–59; Paul Rozin and Edward B. Royzman, "Negativity
    Bias, Negativity Dominance, and Contagion," *Personality and Social Psychology Review* 5, no. 4
    (November 1, 2001): 296–320.

7   Roger Crisp, ed., *Aristotle: Nicomachean Ethics* (London: Cambridge University Press, 2014), 20–22.

8   Martin Seligman, *Authentic Happiness: Using the New Positive Psychology to Realize Your Potential for Lasting Fulfillment* (New York: Simon and Schuster, 2004), 561.

9   James O. Pawelski, "Defining the 'Positive' in Positive Psychology: Part II. A Normative Analysis," *Journal of Positive Psychology* 11, no. 4 (July 3, 2016): 357–365.

10   Tara Brach, *True Refuge: Finding Peace and Freedom in Your Own Awakened Heart* (New York: Bantam, 2012), 61–65.

CHAPTER 5

1   Albert Einstein, "On the Electrodynamics of Moving Bodies," *Annalen der Physik* 17, no. 891 (1905): 50.

2   Gay Hendricks, *The Big Leap* (New York: HarperCollins, 2009), 172.

3   David Allen, *Getting Things Done: The Art of Stress-Free Productivity* (London: Penguin, 2015), 277.

4   Gloria Mark, Daniela Gudith, and Ulrich Klocke, "The Cost of Interrupted Work: More Speed and Stress," *Proceedings of the SIGCHI Conference on Human Factors in Computing Systems* (New York: ACM Digital Library, 2008), 107–110.

5   Sophie Leroy, "Why Is It So Hard to Do My Work? The Challenge of Attention Residue When Switching between Work Tasks," *Organizational Behavior and Human Decision Processes* 109, no. 2 (July 2009): 168–181.

6   W. Warner Burke, "A Perspective on the Field of Organization Development and Change: The Zeigarnik Effect," *Journal of Applied Behavioral Science* 47, no. 2 (June 2011): 143–167.

7   John M. Darley and C. Daniel Batson, "'From Jerusalem to Jericho': A Study of Situational and Dispositional Variables in Helping Behavior," *Journal of Personality and Social Psychology* 27, no. 1 (July 1973): 100–108.

8   Peter Wright, "The Harassed Decision Maker: Time Pressures, Distractions, and the Use of Evidence," *Journal of Applied Psychology* 59, no. 5 (October 1974): 555; Irving L. Janis, "Decision Making under Stress," in *Handbook of Stress*, ed. Leo Goldberger and Solomon Breznitz (New York: The Free Press, 1983), 69–87.

9   Nanna. H. Eller, Bo Netterstrøm, and Åse M. Hansen, "Psychosocial Factors at Home and at Work and Levels of Salivary Cortisol," *Biological Psychology* 73, no. 3 (October 2006): 280–287.

10 Lisa Feldman Barrett, *How Emotions Are Made: The Secret Life of the Brain* (Boston: Houghton Mifflin, 2017), 69.

11 Stephen R. Covey, *The 7 Habits of Highly Effective People: Powerful Lessons in Personal Change* (New York: Simon and Schuster, 2004), 159–164.

12 James E. Loehr and Tony Schwartz, *The Power of Full Engagement: Managing Energy, Not Time, Is the Key to High Performance and Personal Renewal* (New York: Simon and Schuster, 2005), 197–203.

13 Jeffrey S. Durmer and David F. Dinges, "Neurocognitive Consequences of Sleep Deprivation," *Seminars in Neurology*, vol. 25, no. 01 (New York: Thieme Medical, 2005), 117–129; Rachel R. Markwald, Edward L. Melanson, Mark R. Smith, Janine Higgins, Leigh Perreault, Robert H. Eckel, and Kenneth P. Wright, "Impact of Insufficient Sleep on Total Daily Energy Expenditure, Food Intake, and Weight Gain," *Proceedings of the National Academy of Sciences* 110, no. 14 (March 2013): 5695–5700.

14 Patrick J. McGinnis, "You Are the Product: Giancarlo Pitocco and the Attention Economy," May 16, 2019, *FOMO Sapiens*, HBR Presents, podcast, 41:22, https://hbr.org/podcast/2019/05/you-are-the-product-giancarlo-pitocco-and-the-attention-economy.

15 Amy Wrzesniewski and Jane E. Dutton, "Crafting a Job: Revisioning Employees as Active Crafters of Their Work," *Academy of Management Review* 26, no. 2 (April 2001): 179–201.

16 Wrzesniewski and Dutton, 179–201.

17 Allen, *Getting Things Done*, 21.

18 Brian Tracy, *Eat That Frog! 21 Great Ways to Stop Procrastinating and Get More Done in Less Time* (Oakland, CA: Berrett-Koehler Publishers, 2007), 2.

CHAPTER 6

1   Mark Aguiar and Erik Hurst, "Measuring Trends in Leisure: The Allocation of Time over Five Decades," *Quarterly Journal of Economics* 122, no. 3 (August 2007): 969–1006.

2   Ashley V. Whillans, A. C. Weidman, and Elizabeth W. Dunn, "Valuing Time over Money Is Associated with Greater Happiness," *Social Psychological and Personality Science* 7, no. 3 (2016): 213–222.

3   H. E. Hershfield, C. Mogilner, and U. Barnea, "People Who Choose Time over Money Are Happier," *Social Psychological and Personality Science* 7, no. 7 (May 2016): 697–706.

4   Grant E. Donnelly, Tianyi Zheng, Emily Haisley, and Michael I. Norton, "The Amount and Source of Millionaires' Wealth (Moderately) Predict Their Happiness," *Personality and Social Psychology Bulletin* 44, no. 5 (January 11, 2018): 684–699.

5   Daniel Kahneman and Angus Deaton, "High Income Improves Evaluation of Life but Not Emotional Well-Being," *Proceedings of the National Academy of Sciences* 107, no. 38 (August 4, 2010): 16489–16493.

6   Kathleen D. Vohs, "Money Priming Can Change People's Thoughts, Feelings, Motivations, and Behaviors: An Update on 10 Years of Experiments," *Journal of Experimental Psychology: General* 144, no. 4 (August 2015): e86; Kathleen D. Vohs, Nicole L. Mead, and Miranda R. Goode, "The Psychological Consequences of Money," *Science* 314, no. 5802 (November 17, 2006): 1154–1156; Kathleen D. Vohs, N. L. Mead, and M. R. Goode, "Merely Activating the Concept of Money Changes Personal and Interpersonal Behavior," *Current Directions in Psychological Science* 17, no. 3 (June 1, 2008): 208–212.

7   Barry Schwartz, *The Paradox of Choice: Why More Is Less* (New York: Ecco, 2004), loc. 280, Kindle for Mac.

8   Nansook Park, Christopher Peterson, and Martin Seligman, "Strengths of Character and Well Being," *Journal of Social and Clinical Psychology* 23, no. 5 (October 2004): 603–619; Catherine Nelson, "Appreciating Gratitude: Can Gratitude Be Used as a Psychological Intervention to Improve Individual Wellbeing?" *Counselling Psychology Review* 24, nos. 3–4 (November 2009): 38–50; Barbara L. Fredrickson, Michele M. Tugade, Christian E. Waugh, and Gregory R. Larkin, "What Good Are Positive Emotions in Crises? A Prospective Study of Resilience and Emotions Following the Terrorist Attacks on the United States on September 11th, 2001," *Journal of Personality and Social Psychology* 84, no. 2 (February 2003): 365–376.

9   Adam M. Grant and Francesca Gino, "A Little Thanks Goes a Long Way: Explaining Why Gratitude Expressions Motivate Prosocial Behavior," *Journal of Personality and Social Psychology* 98, no. 6 (June 2010): 946.

10 Martin Seligman, Tracy A. Steen, Nansook Park, and Christopher Petersen, "Positive Psychology Progress: Empirical Validation of Interventions," *American Psychologist* 60, no 5 (2005): 879.

11 David Dubois, Derek D. Rucker, and Adam D. Galinsky, "Social Class, Power, and Selfishness: When and Why Upper and Lower Class Individuals Behave Unethically," *Journal of Personality and Social Psychology* 108, no. 3 (March 2015): 436; Francesca Gino and Lamar Pierce, "The Abundance Effect: Unethical Behavior in the Presence of Wealth," *Organizational Behavior and Human Decision Processes* 109, no. 2 (April 24, 2009): 142–155.

12 Daniel Kahneman and Amos Tversky, "Prospect Theory: An Analysis of Decision under Risk," in *Handbook of the Fundamentals of Financial Decision Making: Part I*, ed. Leonard C. MacLean and William T. Ziemba (Hackensack, NJ: World Scientific, 2013), 99–127.

13 Kaitlin Woolley and Ayelet Fishback, "The Experience Matters More Than You Think: People Value Intrinsic Incentives More Inside Than Outside an Activity," *Journal of Personality and Social Psychology* 109, no. 6 (December 2015): 968.

14   Ashley V. Whillans and Elizabeth W. Dunn, "Thinking about Time as Money Decreases Environmental Behavior," *Organizational Behavior and Human Decision Processes* 127 (March 2015): 44–52; Sanford E. DeVoe and Jeffrey Pfeffer, "Hourly Payment and Volunteering: The Effect of Organizational Practices on Decisions about Time Use," *Academy of Management Journal* 50, no. 4 (August 1, 2007): 783-798.

15   "Our Take on the 10 Biggest Frauds in Recent U.S. History," *Forbes*, https://www.forbes.com/pictures/efik45ekdjl/1-enron-2/#55c7c77546d8, accessed March 12, 2019; Joseph L. Bower and Stuart Gilson, "The Social Cost of Fraud and Bankruptcy," *Harvard Business Review*, December 1, 2003, 1–3.

16   Troy Segal, "Enron Scandal: The Fall of a Wall Street Darling," Investopedia, updated May 2019, https://www.investopedia.com/updates/enron-scandal-summary/.

17   "Bernard Ebbers: Billionaire to Prison Inmate," in *Nostalgia and Now*, a blog by Andrew Godfrey, February 9, 2015, https://nostalgia049.wordpress.com/2015/02/09/bernard-ebbers-billionaire-to-prison-inmate/.

18   "From Good to Great...to Below Average," in *Freakanomics Blog* by Steven D. Levitt, July 28, 2008, http://freakonomics.com/2008/07/28/from-good-to-great-to-below-average/; Barry Nielsen, "Fannie Mae, Freddie Mac, and the 2008 Credit Crisis," Investopedia, updated May 20, 2019, https://www.investopedia.com/articles/economics/08/fannie-mae-freddie-mac-credit-crisis.asp.

19   Thomas Li-Ping Tang, Toto Sutarso, Grace Mei-Tzu Wu Davis, Dariusz Dolinski, Abdul Hamid Safwat Ibrahim, and Sharon Lynn Wagner, "To Help or Not to Help? The Good Samaritan Effect and the Love of Money on Helping Behavior," *Journal of Business Ethics* 82, no. 4 (November 2008): 865–87.

20   Philip L. Cooley, Carl M. Hubbard, and Daniel T. Walz, "Retirement Savings: Choosing a Withdrawal Rate That Is Sustainable," *AAII Journal* 10, no. 3 (February 1998): 16–21.

CHAPTER 7

1   "Anatta-lakkhana Sutta: The Discourse on the Not-self Characteristic" (SN 22.59), translated from the Pali by N. K. G. Mendis, *Access to Insight (BCBS Edition)*, June 13, 2010, http://www.accesstoinsight.org/tipitaka/sn/sn22/sn22.059.mend.html

2   Anthony Greenwald, "The Totalitarian Ego: Fabrication and Revision of Personal History," *American Psychologist* 35, no. 7 (July 1980): 603–618.

3   Shunryu Suzuki, *Zen Mind, Beginner's Mind: Informal Talks on Zen Meditation and Practice* (Boston, MA: Shambhala, 2010), 100.

4   John J. Ratey, *Spark: The Revolutionary New Science of Exercise and the Brain* (New York: Little, Brown, 2008), 113–140; Charles H. Hillman, Kirk I. Erickson, and Arthur F. Kramer, "Be Smart, Exercise Your Heart: Exercise Effects on Brain and Cognition," *Nature Reviews Neuroscience* 9, no. 1 (January 2008): 58.

5   Jason Fung, *The Obesity Code: Unlocking the Secrets of Weight Loss* (Vancouver, BC: Greystone Books, 2016), 19.

6   Martin Seligman, *Learned Optimism: How to Change Your Mind and Your Life* (New York: Vintage, 2006), 14–16; Charles P. Martin-Krumm, Philippe G. Sarrazin, Christopher Peterson, and Jean-Pierre Famose, "Explanatory Style and Resilience after Sports Failure," *Personality and Individual Differences* 35, no. 7 (2003): 1685–1695.

7   Michael J. Poulin, Stephanie L. Brown, Peter A. Ubel, Dylan M. Smith, Aleksandra Jankovic, and Kenneth M. Langa, "Does a Helping Hand Mean a Heavy Heart? Helping Behavior and Well-Being among Spouse Caregivers," *Psychology and Aging* 25, no. 1 (March 2010): 108; Carolyn Schwartz, Janice Bell Meisenhelder, Yunsheng Ma, and George Reed, "Altruistic Social Interest Behaviors Are Associated with Better Mental Health," *Psychosomatic Medicine* 65, no. 5 (September 2003): 778–785; Judith A. Wheeler, Kevin M. Gorey, and Bernard Greenblatt, "The Beneficial Effects of Volunteering for Older Volunteers and the People They Serve: A Meta-Analysis," *International Journal of Aging and Human Development* 47, no. 1 (July 1, 1998): 69–79.

8   Adapted from Jack Kornfield, ed., *Teachings of the Buddha* (Boston, MA: Shambhala, 2012), 35–37.

9   Martin Seligman, *Authentic Happiness: Using the New Positive Psychology to Realize Your Potential for Lasting Fulfillment* (New York: Simon and Schuster, 2004), loc. 214, Kindle for Mac.

10 Kristin Neff, *Self-Compassion: The Proven Power of Being Kind to Yourself* (New York: William Morrow, 2011), 41–80.

CHAPTER 8

1   Yuval Noah Harari, *Homo Deus: A Brief History of Tomorrow* (New York: Random House, 2016), 14.

2   Harari, 15.

3   Mateo Hoke, "Michael Pollan: Can Psychedelics Save the World?" *Rolling Stone*, May 15, 2018, https://www.rollingstone.com/culture/culture-features/michael-pollan-can-psychedelics-save-the-world-630231/.

4   Judith Weissman, David Russell, Melanie Jay, Jeannette M. Beasley, Dolores Malaspina, and
     Cheryl Pegus, "Disparities in Health Care Utilization and Functional Limitations among
     Adults with Serious Psychological Distress, 2006–2014," *Psychiatric Services* 68, no. 7 (April 17,
     2017): 653–659.

5   "Suicide Rising across the US," Centers for Disease Control and Prevention, last reviewed
     June 7, 2018, https://www.cdc.gov/vitalsigns/suicide/.

6   Hoke, "Michael Pollan." See also Raffaella Calati, Chiara Ferrari, Marie Brittner, Osmano
     Oasi, Emilie Olié, André F. Carvalho, and Philippe Courtet, "Suicidal Thoughts and Behaviors
     and Social Isolation: A Narrative Review of the Literature," *Journal of Affective Disorders* 245
     (February 15, 2009): 653–667.

7   Nancy Waxler-Morrison, T. Gregory Hislap, Bronwen Mears, and Lisa Kan, "Effects of Social
     Relationships on Survival for Women with Breast Cancer: A Prospective Study," *Social Science
     Medicine* 33, no. 2 (1991): 177–183; Angel Rodriguez-Laso, Maria Victoria Zunzunegui, and
     Angel Otero, "The Effect of Social Relationships on Survival in Elderly Residents of a Southern
     European Community: A Cohort Study," *BMC Geriatriacs* 7, no. 1 (February 2007): 19; Martin
     Pinquart and Paul R. Duberstein, "Association of Social Networks with Cancer Mortality: A
     Meta-analysis," *Critical Review of Oncology Hematology* 75, no. 2 (August 2010): 122–137.

8   John Bowlby, *Attachment and Loss: Vol. 1. Loss* (New York: Basic Books, 1969), 20–23.

9   Harlow, Harry F., Robert O. Dodsworth, and Margaret K. Harlow, "Total Social Isolation in
     Monkeys," *Proceedings of the National Academy of Sciences of the United States of America* 54, no.
     1 (1965): 90.

10   Jane Dutton and Mary Ann Glynn, "Positive Organizational Scholarship," in *The SAGE
     Handbook of Organizational Behavior*, vol. 1, ed. C. Cooper and J. Barling (Thousand Oaks, CA:
     Sage, 2007), 693.

11   Michael Pollan, *How to Change Your Mind: What the New Science of Psychedelics Teaches Us about
     Consciousness, Dying, Addiction, Depression, and Transcendence* (New York: Penguin Books,
     2019), 375–397.

12   Jane E. Dutton and Emily D. Heaphy, "The Power of High-Quality Connections," in *Positive
     Organizational Scholarship: Foundations of a New Discipline*, ed. Kim S. Cameron and Gretchen
     M. Spreitzer (San Francisco: Barrett-Koehler Publishers, 2003), 263–278.

13   Stuart L. Brown, *Play: How It Shapes the Brain, Opens the Imagination, and Invigorates the Soul*
     (New York: Penguin, 2009), 5–15; Mihaly Csikszentmihalyi, *Flow: The Psychology of Optimal
     Experience* (New York: Harper Perennial, 1991), 147–162.

14   Shelly L. Gable, Gian C. Gonzaga, and Amy Strachman, "Will You Be There for Me When
     Things Go Right? Supportive Responses to Positive Event Disclosures," *Journal of Personality
     and Social Psychology* 91, no. 5 (2006): 904.

CHAPTER 9

1   Bhikkhu Ñāṇamoli and Bhikkhu Bodhi, trans., *The Middle Length Discourses of the Buddha: A New Translation of the Majjhima Nikāya* (Somerville, MA: Wisdom Publications, 1995), 534.

2   This story is adapted from David G. Allan, "Who Knows What Is Good or Bad? (My TedEx Talk Transcript)," Medium, September 1, 201, https://medium.com/@@davidgallan/who-knows-what-s-good-or-bad-my-tedx-talk-transcript-8404344779ce

3   Ann Marie Roepke and Martin E. P. Seligman, "Depression and Prospection," *British Journal of Clinical Psychology* 55, no. 1 (2016): 23-48.

4   Alan Watts, *The Wisdom of Insecurity: A Message for an Age of Anxiety* (New York: Pantheon, 1961), 116.

5   Sharon Salzberg, *Faith: Trusting Your Own Deepest Experience* (New York: Riverhead Books, 2002), 44-62.

6   Chris Feudtner, "The Breadth of Hopes," *New England Journal of Medicine* 361, no. 24 (December 2009): 2306-2307.

7   Clayton M. Christensen, *How Will You Measure Your Life?* (Brighton, MA: Harvard Business Review Press, 2017), 6.

8   Alain de Botton, "A Kinder, Gentler Philosophy of Success," 2009, TedEx video, 16:40, https://www.ted.com/talks/alain_de_botton_a_kinder_gentler_philosophy_of_success/transcript?language=en.

9   Daniel Gilbert, *Stumbling on Happiness* (Toronto, ON: Vintage Canada, 2009), 74-90.

10 George T. Doran, "There's a SMART Way to Write Management's Goals and Objectives," *Management Review* 70, no. 11 (1981): 35-36.

11 Gabriele Oettingen, *Rethinking Positive Thinking: Inside the New Science of Motivation* (New York: Penguin Books, 2015), loc. 1768, Kindle for Mac.

12 Carlos Castaneda, *The Teachings of Don Juan: A Yaqui Way of Knowledge* (Oakland, CA: University of California Press, 2016), 45.

13 This exercise is adapted from Stephen Batchelor, *Buddhism without Beliefs: A Contemporary Guide to Awakening* (New York: Riverhead Books, 1998), 28-31.

CHAPTER 10

1   Jon Picoult, "What Went Awry at Wells Fargo? The Beaten Path of a Toxic Culture," *The New York Times*, October 8, 2016, https://www.nytimes.com/2016/10/09/jobs/what-went-awry-at-wells-fargo-the-beaten-path-of-a-toxic-culture.html.

2   Nicola Bianchi and Franco Fiordelisi, "Measuring and Assessing Risk Culture," in *Risk Culture in Banking*, ed. Alessandro Carretta, Paola Schwizer, and Franco Fiordelisi (Cham, Switzerland: Palgrave Macmillan Studies in Banking and Financial Institutions, 2017), 155-176.

3   Kim Cameron, *Positive Leadership: Strategies for Extraordinary Performance* (San Francisco: Berrett-Koehler, 2012), loc. 202, Kindle for Mac.

CPSIA information can be obtained
at www.ICGtesting.com
Printed in the USA
FFHW021022151119
56059340-62049FF

9 781544 504827